FROM

WALKING TOURS

San Francisco

2nd Edition

Lisa Legarde

MACMILLAN • USA

ABOUT THE AUTHOR:

Lisa Legarde was born in New Orleans and graduated from Wellesley College with a B.A. in English. She has traveled extensively and is the author of *Frommer's Walking Tours: Paris.* She is also the author of several other Frommer's guides.

MACMILLAN TRAVEL

A Simon & Schuster Macmillan Company
1633 Broadway
New York, NY 10019

ISBN: 0-02-860472-5
ISSN: 1081-3403

Editor and Map Editor: Douglas Stallings
Design by Amy Peppler Adams—designLab, Seattle
Digital Cartography by Ortelius Design and Devorah Wilkenfeld

SPECIAL SALES

Manufactured in the United States of America

CONTENTS

LIST OF MAPS

The Walking Tours

An Invitation to the Reader

In researching this book, I discovered many wonderful places. I'm sure you'll find others. Please tell us about them, so we can share the information with your fellow travelers in upcoming editions. If you were disappointed with a recommendation, I'd love to know that, too. Please write to:

Lisa Legarde
Frommer's Walking Tours: San Francisco
Macmillan Travel
1633 Broadway
New York, NY 10019

An Additional Note

Please be advised that travel information is subject to change at any time. The authors, editors, and publisher cannot be held responsible for the experiences of readers while traveling. Your safety is important to us, however, so we encourage you to stay alert and be aware of your surroundings. Keep a close eye on cameras, purses, and wallets, all favorite targets of thieves and pickpockets.

Introducing San Francisco

Some people who have never visited San Francisco before might wonder why any sane person would want to live in a place where underground rumblings threaten to one day dump the entire city into the ocean. But after you've walked the tours in this book chances are you'll wonder why anyone *wouldn't* want to live here. And you'll understand why Tony Bennett sings, "I left my heart in San Francisco."

Anyone visiting the Bay Area today has to be struck by the friendliness and ease of the city's people. It is a wonder that an urban environment where storekeepers and others speak to you and inquire about your well-being still exists in this country. It is a city of civility. Some find this strange and unnerving at first, but it doesn't take long to grow accustomed to such graciousness.

San Francisco is a difficult place to categorize. It has an almost small-town feel but is a city of almost 750,000 and the hub of a major metropolitan area with a population of almost six million—the sixth largest in the country. While the rest of California is turning increasingly Republican, San Francisco remains a Democratic stronghold.

1

Surrounded by some of the most conservative communities in the state, San Francisco is an island of liberalism (with certain conservative beachheads). This live-and-let-live attitude goes far back in San Francisco's gold rush roots, and has carried through to more modern times. In the last forty years, the city has been at the vanguard of several progressive social movements, including the rise of the Beats in the '50s, the hippie culture of the '60s, and the Gay Rights movement of the '70s. Today the utopian dream persists, aided and abetted by the bewitching physical beauty of the city.

While it is increasingly assaulted by urban social problems such as drugs, crime, racism, poverty, and homelessness, San Francisco tries to grapple with these problems by keeping in mind their human aspect. Not that this is not a city of monumental political struggles. Conflicts sometimes seem to overwhelm the city, such as the impact of urban renewal and gentrification on deteriorating neighborhoods, the difficulty balancing development and environmental protection, and always the fight against growing intolerance. Today more than ever, it seems, the strains are showing. Only after thirty years of wrangling has the new Center for the Arts at Yerba Buena Gardens opened on Mission Street in the SoMa district; the city that has been identified as the premier gay oasis in the nation is under assault from anti-gay talk show hosts and others who want to turn back the clock; and the shipping industry and major corporations are moving out, trying to get away from big-city problems. Further, a narrow single-interest politics has made the debate on these issues increasingly strident.

But in so many ways San Francisco is a city unlike any other in the United States. Despite their conflicts, San Franciscans seem to share a zest for life. As many disasters have shown, they do bounce back from adversity. And even in a stagnating California economy, exciting projects are opening up, such as the new Museum of Modern Art and the long-awaited Yerba Buena Gardens next door. You'll be excited by San Francisco, and the best way to find out how is to walk around and meet its inhabitants. Your trip to San Francisco won't be cheap (though you'll also find some bargains), but I also think you'll find that it's worth every penny. Built on 43 hills facing the Pacific Ocean, with some of the most fabulous views and interesting architecture on the west coast, lively and diverse, it remains one of this country's most enchanting travel destinations.

SOME HISTORY

Now that I've described how the city looks and feels today, I thought you might be curious as to how it got that way. Although most of what you will see on these twelve walking tours didn't exist before the mid-1800s, San Francisco does have a long and interesting history. And a basic familiarity with that history will help to put our walking tour stops into a more meaningful context.

The Beginnings

San Francisco's earliest known inhabitants were tribes of the Coast Miwok Indians, who lived primarily to the north of the area upon which the city grew, and the Costanoans (derived from the Spanish *costanos,* meaning "coast people"), who lived to the south and east of the city. When they lived here, San Francisco was nothing more than a series of sand dunes. But until the Spanish arrived, their community was thriving.

It wasn't until 1775 that Spanish sailor Juan Ayala, while on a mapping expedition for the Spanish, actually sailed through the Golden Gate into San Francisco Bay. By the next year the Spanish were ready to begin a colony. In 1776 Captain Juan Bautista de Anza walked from Mexico to San Francisco with his lieutenant, José Morega; Francisco Palou, a priest; and thirty-four families to establish a *presidio* (or fortress), and a mission. They set up the Presidio on June 27, 1776, on a hill overlooking San Francisco Bay. Two days later, Mission Dolores (see Tour 12, Stop 15) was established, and on June 29, 1776, Father Junipero Serra held the first mass for the colonists. The building, finished in 1791, still functions as Mission Dolores and is the oldest standing building in San Francisco.

The future of the natives there was not so fortunate. Permanent Spanish settlement brought diseases against which the native Costanoans had no natural immunity, and thousands died. Others were held captive and forced into heavy labor while the Spanish attempted to convert them to Christianity. When Mexico won its independence from Spain in 1821, the missions were broken up by the government. But the Costanoans, finally freed, died out on their own land, which had long since grown foreign to them.

Yerba Buena

Soon after Mexico's break from Spanish rule, many Californios (as the region's early ranching families were called) settled on government land grants in the San Francisco area and began very profitable, bountiful lives. They began selling hides cured on their ranches to various passing ships, and it wasn't long before a real trade market developed, bringing other Europeans, particularly the English and French, to San Francisco Bay.

In 1822 a British seaman, William Richardson jumped ship while on one of these trading missions because he'd fallen in love with the Presidio commandante's daughter, Dona Maria Antonia Martinez. The commandante didn't trust Richardson and refused to allow them to marry. Hoping to get the commandante to change his mind, Richardson converted to Catholicism and was baptized at Mission Dolores. Nevertheless, his devotion to Dona Maria Antonia Martinez was unflagging, and he remained in the Bay Area where he began teaching sailing, carpentry, and navigation to the Mexicans. For two years he worked hard and was finally able to build himself a ship. He christened it the *Maria Antonia*. The commandante finally relented and gave the couple his blessing when it became clear to him that Richardson had every intention of remaining in the Bay Area and that his educational efforts were bringing prosperity to the community.

By the 1830s trading was so heavy in the Bay Area that Richardson asked the commandante for permission to build a home and start his own colony. Permission was granted, and in the place he called simply Yerba Buena (or "good herb") after a mint plant that grew wild in the area, he erected a simple lean-to (later a wooden shack) very near today's Montgomery Street. It was out of that shack that Richardson began his own hide trade, eventually becoming the port's first harbormaster. As he grew wealthier Richardson replaced the shack with an adobe structure that he called Casa Grande. He has gone down in San Francisco's history as the city's first "merchant prince."

Not long afterward, Jacob Leese, an Ohioan, stretched a tarp over four posts, becoming Richardson's first neighbor and his first competitor. More settlers followed, and by 1839 a veritable little town with a main street down the center had grown up around Casa Grande. The first saloon was opened by Jean-Jacques Vioget, who was inspired by the potential he saw in the healthy and quickly growing Yerba Buena. Vioget also surveyed the land, drew up a map of the town, and laid out the central plaza.

In 1846, during the Mexican War, U.S. Marines landed in Yerba Buena and raised the American flag over Yerba Buena's plaza. They named it Portsmouth Square—after their ship, the U.S.S. *Portsmouth*. In 1847 Yerba Buena was renamed San Francisco, and since its population had increased so dramatically, the town hired Jasper O'Farrel, an Irish sailor, to extend Vioget's original grid plan. When the United States won the war with Mexico the following year, California became an American territory.

The Gold Rush

San Francisco was growing steadily, and by April 1848 its population had reached approximately 1,000. There were shops, warehouses, a couple of hotels, and several saloons. People were living as comfortably as conditions would permit, and they enjoyed the slow growth of their town. Newcomers, who arrived by ship or in covered wagons, were welcomed, but no one could have imagined the changes that were about to take place.

In January of 1849 John W. Marshall, who was building a sawmill for Swiss Captain John Sutter (who wished to found a Swiss-American settlement on the Sacramento River), discovered some small particles of gold in the American River. Sutter asked Marshall to keep news of the discovery to himself for fear that the land would be destroyed by fortune hunters and sought the advice of his friend Sam Brannan, one of the first Americans to arrive in San Francisco after the Mexican War. Brannan tried to allay Sutter's fears, and for a month nothing was said about the discovery of gold. That was because Brannan was busy opening and stocking shops with food and mining implements, in preparation for the pandemonium that would follow his announcement of "Gold! Gold!" as he ran through Portsmouth Square. He followed up with an announcement in his newspaper, the *California Star*.

No one could resist the prospect of becoming instantly rich. Shop owners hung signs reading "Gone to the Diggings" in their windows, small ships set sail for the gold strike, nearly sinking with the weight of mining materials, and other townspeople left their homes after having loaded up their mules, wagons, and horses with supplies. Daily business stopped; ships stood like ghosts, their crews gone, their cargoes partially loaded or unloaded; and construction stopped dead. News of the gold strike traveled quickly around the world.

Not everyone headed for the hills. A couple of shrewd merchants realized that there was money to be made in trade, and they bought up entire ships' cargoes without even knowing what they held. Ships' captains auctioned off cargoes for as much as ten times their worth, and merchants sold supplies, food, and tools at prices that might be shocking even today. A pair of boots might cost forty dollars. Eggs that were shipped around Cape Horn cost ten dollars a dozen, and those from California might cost as much as three or four dollars each. Drinking water cost a dollar a bucket, and someone once paid a whopping $600 for a barrel of flour. The restaurant business boomed because most people were far from family, hearth, and home-cooking.

Many struck it instantly rich. One man dug up $50,000 worth of gold in only a few days. Another unearthed gold worth $17,000. Still another absentmindedly kicked at some rocks by his front door and turned up $2,000 worth. The biggest nugget ever found, at twenty-three pounds, was likely the driving force that continued to draw men West, many of them not as solid as the original citizens of Yerba Buena.

Australian penal colonies sent ships to California from Sydney and Hobart Town. The French sent boatloads of prostitutes to take advantage of the shortage of women in the San Francisco area. One writer reports that the "scrapings of hell and bedlam converged on San Francisco."

Some of those scrapings joined a gang of "roughs" called the Hounds, who hailed from various Pacific ports or had deserted their regiments during the Mexican War. In 1849 the Hounds appointed themselves the city's justice committee. In a tent called "Tammany Hall" they held their first meeting to decide what "injustices" they should correct; their first mission would be to drive out a group of Chileans and Peruvians who lived in the area. They killed some and raped many, and for weeks the Hounds terrorized communities of foreigners. Finally, they began to demand protection money. But because they were attacking "fringe" groups on the outskirts of town, most people didn't take much notice of the havoc wreaked by the Hounds until they began attacking people in the center of San Francisco.

When Sam Brannan and a group of men finally decided to take the law into their own hands, they ran the Hounds out of town in just one day. The Hounds didn't go far, however, because another group of n'er-do-wells, the Sydney Ducks, took them in.

The Barbary Coast

The Ducks ruled the waterfront, then known as "Sydney Town," after the growing number of Australian prisoners who had settled there. Sydney Town grew up under the leadership of David C. Broderick, an Irishman. A small man with sloping shoulders, a heavy black beard, and thin hard lips, Broderick built a "crime machine" and prostitutes and criminals came from all over the world to live there. After an unidentified sailor walked through Sydney Town and called it the "Barbary Coast," after the pirate coast of North Africa, everyone began referring to the area bounded by Clay, Commercial, Chinatown, and Broadway by that name. For forty years this section of town thrived, becoming the home of every harlot, thief, murderer, dirty politician, and fugitive living in San Francisco in the mid-1800s. At one time there were 3,000 drinking establishments—an average of one saloon for every 95 people.

The Sydney Ducks and others who lived in the Barbary Coast practically took over the streets of San Francisco. They robbed indiscriminately and beat many a man senseless. One of their most common practices was also San Francisco's most infamous form of lawlessness—drugging or knocking out sailors who had just arrived in the port for a little rest and relaxation, then selling them to ships bound for the Far East. Originally, and most frequently, the destination was Shanghai, China, which is why this practice became widely known as "shanghaiing."

Perhaps the most destructive of the Ducks' deeds were the six fires set between Christmas Eve 1849 and June 22, 1851. The first came early that morning as a complete surprise to sleepy San Franciscans who suddenly realized that they had no fire department. In spite of a valiant effort to douse the flames, most of the town burned, and the buildings the fire hadn't destroyed were looted or ruined by the Sydney Ducks. Another fire was set in May 1850, destroying over three square blocks and killing one of San Francisco's most beloved citizens, Captain Vincente, who died trying to help people out of burning buildings. The furious residents offered a $5,000 reward for any information about who started the blaze, and a fire company was officially formed.

Another fire only a month later prompted new rules citywide. The digging of artesian wells was required, and each home was to keep six buckets of water on hand. There was also a $500 fine for refusing to fight fires. And in September their plan was tested when another fire began. This time, when the city rose yet again from the ashes its residents adopted the Phoenix as the city seal.

Some preachers saw the fires as a sign, comparing San Francisco to Sodom, and insisted that the city would continue to burn as long as its citizens persisted in sinning. As the city degenerated further, some began to think the preachers might be right. The city was becoming overrun with rats, an unwanted import carried in on ships from around the world. Attempts to exterminate them led to pollution of the water supply. Furthermore, the city streets were becoming dangerous, muddy bogs. So bad were they that people could sink to their deaths if they weren't careful. Though attempts to pave the roads were made, not much was accomplished because greedy gold miners were unwilling to part with any of their newfound wealth. Instead of imposing some kind of citywide tax, officials posted signs reading THIS STREET IS IMPASSABLE. NOT EVEN JACKASSABLE.

Nearly a year went by without a major fire, and residents had grown comfortable as the city rebuilt. When the Sydney Ducks threatened to set the worst fire yet, most people didn't take them seriously. They should have. The fire they set on May 4, 1851, destroyed 19 square blocks in two hours.

San Franciscans came to believe that law enforcement agencies were ineffective, so they took matters into their own hands. They called for Sam Brannan because of his prior success in running The Hounds out of town. Brannan climbed atop his soapbox and spoke convincingly about the virtues of a Vigilance Committee, and only minutes after he stepped down hundreds of men were prepared to sign up. They vowed to hang the next man who committed a crime.

Apparently John Jenkins didn't believe them because shortly thereafter he marched right into a store and marched right back out carrying the safe. Although he was grinning then, he stopped smiling when he was captured by the Vigilance Committee and became the first man hanged. Sam Brannan yelled, "Every lover of liberty and good order lay hold the rope!"

What little government the city had was hopelessly corrupt, and there were few who had the gumption to criticize. One crusader at the time was James King William, only 26 years old when he bought the *Daily Evening Bulletin*. He threatened (in the newspaper) to rout out the city's corrupt politicians. William was angry that James Casey was allowed a position on the Board of Supervisors of San Francisco, even though he had spent two years in Sing Sing. He was also furious that the jail keeper, Billy Mulligan (who had been a New York hooligan), had taken it upon himself to set imprisoned criminals free. There had been over 1,000 murders and no one hanged in a year. In an editorial William claimed that he was going to "make certain parties writhe under the agony to which his exposures would subject them," and writhe they did. The *Bulletin* received threats from these parties and William published them on the front page to boost circulation.

William got even more deeply involved in city politics when Charles Cora, a gambler who had shot U.S. Marshall William A. Richardson, came to trial. King believed that jailer Billy Mulligan would let Cora walk free; the *Bulletin* screamed that if Cora did, the city should "HANG BILLY MULLIGAN." William even went so far as to suggest hanging the sheriff, too, if Mulligan let Cora go.

Shortly after this episode, in yet another article, he attacked James Casey. Judge MacGowan, also a criminal, went to Casey telling him that James King William had libeled him. Casey headed straight for the *Bulletin*'s office but was thrown out. When King emerged, Casey shot him.

King's martyrdom in 1856 drew the Vigilance Committee together once again. Some 8,000 members met in a building they called Fort Gunnybags on Sacramento Street. They captured and hung Casey and Cora, but Mulligan (who they had also captured) escaped by disguising himself as a priest.

With some of the crime problem under control, immigrants became the focus of further turmoil in San Francisco. The Chinese, who were immigrating in great numbers and were willing to work for much lower wages than their American counterparts, were creating a labor glut. When they disembarked from the ships the Chinese immigrants were led directly to the Portsmouth Square area. Once the center of town, it was by then being used as a buffer zone between the Barbary Coast and the city's more respectable neighborhoods. San Franciscans didn't know that Chinatown, with its "Daughters of Joy" import business, tongs, and opium trade would prove to be almost as great a problem as the Barbary Coast.

The Late 1800s

Following the Civil War, San Francisco, which supported the Union—though not in a very active way, underwent a period of normal prosperity and growth. Immigrants continued to arrive, particularly Italians. They joined the French, Irish, and Chinese, who had already established large communities in the city proper. The Italians began settling at North Beach, starting fishing businesses and restaurants and soon established themselves as a financial strength to be reckoned with.

On April 14, 1860, the first Pony Express rider arrived with letters after a one-and-a-half-day trip from Missouri, and the Pacific Telegraph was completed in 1861. Soon afterwards, Leland Stanford, Collis P. Huntington, Mark Hopkins, and Charles Crocker—known collectively as the "Big Four"—began working on the Central Pacific (later Southern Pacific) Railroad, which would soon join with the Union Pacific to create the first transcontinental railroad. On May 8, 1869, the last spike, a gold one, joining the Union Pacific was driven in Promontory Point, Utah.

By 1874 the Central Pacific Railroad was carrying all the mail, huge numbers of passengers, and freight across the country. Previously all of this type of transport was done by ship, much of it by the Pacific Mail shipping company. The ruthless Big Four began to drive Pacific Mail and other small companies out of business. This competition naturally led to rate wars, the first of which was between Pacific Mail and Central Pacific. Pacific Mail made a valiant effort to stop the inevitable, but to no avail. The government was forced to step in and guarantee Pacific Mail a fixed monthly income. Unfortunately, other smaller businesses didn't fare nearly as well. The Big Four were creating a transportation monopoly and were getting richer and richer.

With their fortunes, they retreated to the top of Nob Hill to build extravagant mansions. And they were joined there by the men who made their fortunes in silver from the Comstock Lode. Lumber, coal, restaurant, and hotel businesses boomed, and the city's population doubled between 1870 and 1875.

Even with the city's growing prosperity, there was unrest, some of it directed toward the rich on top of Nob Hill, some closer to the bottom. Irishman Dennis Kearny, who had already been jailed briefly for storming Nob Hill with a mob, shouting, "I say down with the rich hell-hounds," turned his discontent against the Chinese. This time, he led a mob to the docks where hundreds of Chinese immigrants were disembarking, claiming that the "coolies" were coming to San Francisco to glut the depressed labor market. The riots lasted three days. Eventually, the rioters were chased away from the docks, but that didn't stop them from continuing attacks against the Chinese (as well as the Pacific Mail and Central Pacific, the first companies to utilize the cheaper Chinese labor). The protests and violence continued until the Chinese Exclusion Act was passed in 1882.

Not long after the Chinese Exclusion Act was passed, people began to search for ways to free themselves of the high-priced railroad transport and they started overland wagon trade transportation. Other attempts were made to carry merchandise by sea around Cape Horn, but no one could seem to break the stronghold of the railroad company. Finally, in 1891 the Traffic Association was formed for the purpose of creating more water transportation. Two steamer lines were formed as competition, and many merchants boycotted the railroad. It became clear that it was much cheaper to trade by ship than it was by rail, and for a while shippers were able to save millions of dollars. Even the newspapers joined in the fight against the Big Four.

During this period in San Francisco history, people were living the high life. Much of the socializing centered around the Montgomery Block (see Tour 3, Stop 2 for more). Ambrose Bierce, Mark Twain, George Sterling, and Ina Donna Coolbrith were some of the very first members of the exclusive Bohemian Club, which was also founded at this time. San Francisco, in spite of the Barbary Coast reputation and its high crime rate, was in its Golden Age, growing culturally as well as financially. Its rough edges were being smoothed out, and a sense of San Francisco style developed. It was during this period that San Francisco's famous Victorian architecture arose as well. People were settling comfortably into a city that all felt was destined to be great.

The Great Quake

In 1906, disaster struck the city. On April 18 at 5:13am, San Francisco was shaken awake by the most powerful earthquake ever recorded in the 48 contiguous states. The city's 400,000 inhabitants were incredulous. The earth seemed to be moving in waves, rolling and splitting right before their very eyes. The quake set off a series of fires that grew into one huge conflagration and blazed across the city. Fire companies were helpless against the fire because water mains had broken, and they were unable to harness the eighty thousand gallons that rushed along the streets. No matter what anybody did the fire raged and raged, swallowing hundreds of beautiful redwood Victorians as it ran up and down the city's hills.

That same day, as residents realized that the whole city would soon be consumed by fire, they began moving outside the city limits, dragging their children, pets, and trunks full of belongings behind them. Out of desperation firemen even tried dumping sewer water on the flames, but to no avail. The fire swept South of Market Street and headed for San Francisco's fashionable Palace Hotel as survivors were forced to take refuge under tents.

The second day, as fire climbed Nob Hill and engulfed the half-finished Fairmont Hotel, San Francisco's wealthiest also fled, taking with them as much as they could load onto wagons, including paintings they had cut from their frames and rolled up. They began to realize that something had to be done to stop the fire before it reached Van Ness Avenue. City officials came up with a plan for dynamiting buildings ahead of the fire so there would be nothing to burn and the blaze would extinguish itself. As the fire came within four blocks of Van Ness, the order was given to light the dynamite. Before the dust cleared it was evident that the plan had worked. The fire had been turned back into itself and would burn out. It had taken three days to extinguish the blaze; over 28,000 buildings were destroyed and 500 people were killed.

Despite the many dead and the great property loss, some good did come of the fire. Ironically, it wiped out the entire Barbary Coast. Finally, San Francisco was rid of the troublesome area of town, and the city would be able to rebuild without the dens of iniquity that lined the Barbary Coast and the streets of Chinatown. Once again, the Phoenix would rise.

Six days after the fire, ships were again able to sail from the port of San Francisco, and restaurants were rebuilding. Restaurant owners adopted the slogan, "Eat, drink, and be merry, for tomorrow we may have to go to Oakland." One particularly optimistic restaurateur, "Poppa" Coppa, whose restaurant had been burned to the ground, cooked a huge meal in the ruins of his former kitchen. Ironically, one of the buildings spared was The Hotaling Warehouse, which was stocked with whisky at the time of the fire. Groups of people watched as other burned-out buildings in the business district were being dismantled and trucked away, and as they watched they sang:

> *If, as they say, God sparked the town*
> *For being over-frisky—*
> *Why did He burn all the churches down*
> *And spare Hotaling's whisky?*

Good-natured and optimistic, San Franciscans soon began building a newer and more modern city. After the dust settled, the federal and state governments extended unlimited credit to San Francisco. Hotels and restaurants were rebuilt, theaters reopened, and electrically powered streetcars were installed all over the city as replacements for the cable car lines that had been destroyed. A new city government was put in place, and on February 20, 1915, San Franciscans held the Panama Pacific Exposition as a show of the city's renewed vitality. The Exposition hosted more visitors than the city had ever seen, and businesses were prospering once again. World War I had only just begun.

The World Wars & the Depression

Though San Franciscans were nervous about the war, it didn't really touch them until July 22, 1916. During the Preparedness Day parade of 50,000 people, a bomb went off, killing nine and wounding over a hundred others. The bomber was never found, although two innocent men were arrested.

In April 1917 the United States declared war on Germany, and San Francisco took part immediately when the city seized four German ships in the San Francisco Bay just off Sausalito. Residents took part in meetings, bonfires, and parades in a loud display of patriotism; 11,000 men were drafted and headed out to fight in Europe; and shipbuilding businesses prospered as the building of wooden ships gave way to the construction of a fleet of steel. Finally, on November 11, 1918, news of the Armistice came and San Franciscans celebrated with flag waving, singing, and more bonfires.

Afterward, yet another period of prosperity was enjoyed by the city of San Francisco, but it came to an unfortunate and abrupt end with the stock market crash of 1929. Businesses failed, but spirited San Franciscans tried to hold on. In May of 1930 the San Francisco longshoremen staged a walk-out that would go down as the largest strike in the history of the country. The city was immobilized by the strike for four days and before the longshoremen's demands were met, riots rocked the city. By 1931 San Francisco really felt the grip of the Depression, which had already inflicted deep suffering on the rest of the nation.

Fortunately the Depression left San Francisco early, and the outbreak of World War II spurred another period of growth. Shipyards prospered as the demand for warships grew, and 500,000 men left San Francisco to protect U.S. interests. Among them were 33,000 Japanese Americans, who fought in the war despite the way they had been treated by the U.S. government—shortly after the war broke out, they had been imprisoned in camps.

Bohemia on the Bay

In the 1950s San Francisco became a haven for America's Beat Generation a group of free-spirited poets who challenged the materialism and conformity of American society by embracing anarchy and Eastern philosophy. The Beats flourished in the city's open-minded climate. They wore black and hung out in the coffeehouses and bars of North Beach where rents were low and cheap wine plentiful. Herb Caen, a columnist for the *San Francisco Chronicle*, thought the Beats were from out of this world and likened them to Sputnik. The comparison resulted in the term *beatnik*. Ginsberg, Corso, and Kerouac, from New York City, came west and joined Ferlinghetti, Rexroth, Snyder, and the Beat movement gained national attention. A major event was Ginsberg's reading of *Howl* at the Six Gallery in the Marina district on October 13, 1955 (see Tour 3, Stop 10). Ferlinghetti published the poem in 1956, but customs seized it, and the police arrested and charged Ferlinghetti and his bookstore manager with obscenity. A trial followed, but the judge ruled that the poem had redeeming social value, thereby reaffirming the rights of all Americans to freedom of expression. A year later Jack Kerouac published *On the Road*, the other bible of the Beats.

At that time, North Beach was the center of the city's night life. Two clubs of note were the hungry i and the Purple Onion (see Tour 3, Stops 7 and 8), where everyone who was anyone or became anyone on the entertainment scene made an appearance. Mort Sahl, Dick Gregory, Lenny Bruce, Barbra Streisand, and Woody Allen all played the hungry i, and Maya Angelou even appeared as a singer and dancer at the Purple Onion. North Beach was the center of bohemian life in the '50s, but it all came to a rapid end when tour buses started rolling in, rents went up, and Broadway was turned into a sex club strip in the late '50s and early '60s. The Beats moved on, and the alternative scene shifted to Berkeley and San Francisco's Haight Street.

The torch passed from the Beats and North Beach to the hippies and the Haight, but it cast a very different light indeed. In place of the Beats' angst, anarchy, negativism, nihilism, and poetry came the love, communalism, openness, Mother Earth philosophies, drugs, and rock music of the hippies. Although the scent of marijuana was palpable everywhere—on the streets, in the cafes, in Golden Gate Park—the real drugs of choice were LSD (a tab of good acid cost $5) and other hallucinogenics. At that time, LSD was legal, and scientists like Timothy Leary were experimenting with its effects and exhorting the youth to "turn on, tune in, and drop out."

Poetry readings had given way to concerts at the Fillmore or the Avalon Ballroom where hippies went to the first Family Dog Rock 'n' Roll Dance and Concert. A tribute to Dr. Strange, featuring Jefferson Airplane, the Marbles, the Great Society, and the Charlatans, was given at the Longshoreman's Hall near Fisherman's Wharf in 1965. At this event, which turned out to be the first major event of the '60s, Allen Ginsberg led a snake dance through the crowd. In January 1966 the three-day Trips Festival, organized by rock promoter Bill Graham was also held at the Longshoreman's Hall. The climax of the festival was the appearance of Ken Kesey and the Merry Pranksters Acid Test Show in which Kesey appeared in a space suit while his sidekick, Neal Cassady, played the role of the driver of the Prankster bus and swung out repeatedly over the crowd.

The Summer of Love followed in 1967 as thousands of young people streamed into the city in search of drugs and sex. The hippies were generally under 25, and they constituted the first youth movement to take over the nation and ironically became the first generation of young, independent, and moneyed consumers to be courted by the corporate world. Ultimately the hippie movement deteriorated, and the Haight began to draw a fringe group of crazies like Charles Manson, leaving only a legacy of sex, drugs, violence, and consumerism.

The 1970s brought a series of stormy events, including the kidnapping of Patty Hearst in 1974; the mass suicide in Jonestown, Guyana, of a group of San Franciscans who belonged to Jim Jones's People's Temple; and most importantly, the beginning of the gay rights movement.

The Committee for Homosexual Freedom was created in San Francisco in the spring of 1969 following the raid on the Stonewall in New York City. That fall, a protest against *San Francisco Examiner* columnist Robert Patterson erupted into a confrontation with police and concluded with a sit-in at the Mayor Calioto's office.

For the next several years gays openly protested national and local organizations for discriminating against homosexuals. Groups targeted included the American Psychiatric Association, which held its 1970 convention in San Francisco. The National Gay Liberation conference was also held in San Francisco that year, and Charles Thorp, argued for the use of what he felt was the more positive, celebratory "gay" instead of homosexual. The first National Gay Celebration Day and Gay Pride Week were also held that year.

Harvey Milk, owner of a camera store in the Castro, became the first openly gay person to hold public office—a seat on the San Francisco Board of Supervisors. Together, he and liberal Mayor George Moscone developed a positive gay rights agenda, but in 1978 both were killed by Dan White, a former Supervisor. White, a Catholic and former policeman who espoused the family values of his blue collar Irish background, hated the liberal policies of Milk and Moscone. After successfully arguing that his junk food diet led to his unstable mental state, White was convicted of manslaughter, not murder, and was sentenced to five years. On that day, angry and grieving, the gay community rioted, overturning and burning police cars in a night of rage. To this day a candlelight vigil is held on November 27. After his release, White moved to Los Angeles and committed suicide. The whole story was recently made into an opera.

In the early 1980s AIDS came. The hedonistic lifestyle that had played out in the discos, bars, baths, and streets changed as the seriousness of the epidemic sunk in and the dying increased. Political efforts shifted, the community demanding more money for social services and research to deal with the AIDS crisis. Unfortunately, AIDS has also brought a backlash against the community, with an increase in gay bashing and hate crimes. Nevertheless, the gay community in San Francisco remains strong and politically powerful.

In 1989 San Francisco was again shaken by a huge quake. The city suffered a great deal of damage, but not as much as from the 1906 quake. And the city has rebuilt and revitalized itself in the last few years. This latest disaster is sure not to be the last, but city residents have come to accept these rumblings as part of life—not even an earthquake can shake them from their faith that there is no finer place to live than the "City by the Bay."

As you walk up and down San Francisco's hills, you'll enjoy its almost Mediterranean quality and sprawling panoramas (such as the views from the top of Telegraph Hill or Nob Hill); it will come as no surprise that artists and writers have always flocked to San Francisco. Many of the tours will take you to the former homes and hangouts of various well-known (and not-so-well-known) literary and artistic figures. Others will direct you to some of San Francisco's finest and proudest Painted Ladies—the city's ornately decorated Victorian homes. You'll also have the opportunity to visit San Francisco's ethnic communities when you take tours of North Beach, Chinatown, Japantown, and the Mission District. And when you get tired of climbing hills you can always take a leisurely stroll through San Francisco's playground, Golden Gate Park.

The Tours at a Glance

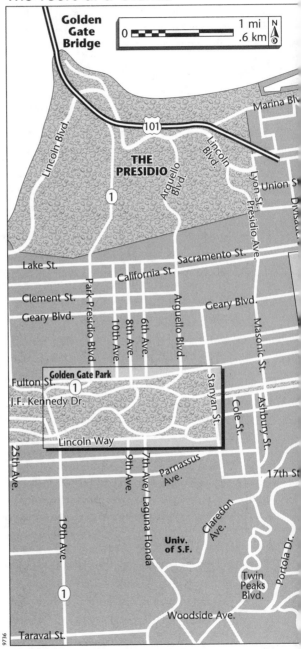

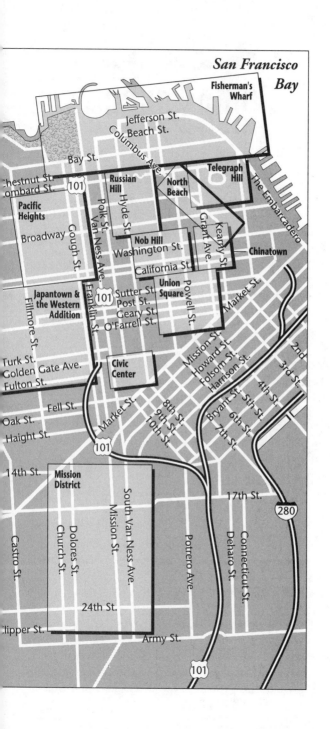

UNION SQUARE

Start: Corner of Taylor and O'Farrell streets.

Public Transportation: 27 Bryant bus to the corner of Taylor and O'Farrell streets.

Finish: Market and Fifth streets (Hallidie Plaza).

Time: 3 hours.

Best Times: Any time the shops are open.

Worst Times: Big holidays when shopping centers are closed.

Hills That Could Kill: None.

The Union Square area is, in my opinion, the best place to begin exploring San Francisco. You can do a little sightseeing, perhaps a little shopping, become acquainted with the public transportation system, and make a trip to the San Francisco Convention and Visitor's Bureau.

Union Square is located just above Market Street and is San Francisco's theater and shopping center. The central square is surrounded by such landmarks as the Westin St. Francis Hotel and retail giants Macy's and Hermès, just to name a couple. The neighborhood is like New York's Broadway and Fifth Avenue all rolled into one—only a lot cleaner, and frequented by locals and tourists alike.

Take your time, and indulge yourself a little. Compared with the rest of the city, Union Square is fairly flat. I'm starting you out easy. Consider it pre-season training.

• • • • • • • • • • • • • • • •

Head up Taylor Street and cross Geary Street. Go right on Geary, looking for 445 Geary Street, the:

1. **Curran Theater,** built in 1922 of reinforced concrete and one of the city's main theaters. Note the mansard roof and the metal sign frames. This is the main theater for the Best of Broadway series. But if you're going to pay good money to see the show, you should make sure you don't get stuck too far back in the balconies because the acoustics are less than acceptable up there.

Also, on the right, but a bit farther along at 415 Geary Street you'll see the:

2. **Geary Theater.** Built in 1909, it was originally called the Columbia Theater, and its most interesting exterior features are the multicolored terra-cotta columns with fruits and garlands. Also note the masks of comedy and tragedy on opposite sides of the doorway. Usually the home of the American Conservatory Theater (ACT), the Geary was badly damaged in the 1989 earthquake and is still under repair. In fact, the theater was scheduled to reopen in 1993, but at press time it was still closed.

When you get to the corner of Geary and Mason streets, cross to the side of Geary on which the theaters are located and head back in the direction of Taylor Street. On the left at the corner of Taylor Street is the:

3. **Four Seasons Clift Hotel,** at 491–99 Geary Street. Built just before the Panama Pacific International Exposition in 1915 for lawyer Frederick Clift (who had a suite designed especially for himself), this hotel is one of San Francisco's most elegant. A 240-room addition was completed in 1926. Today there are 329 guest rooms.

Go inside and have a look at the collection of modern and contemporary art in the lobby. If you're interested in the hotel's original decor, ask someone at the desk to point you in the direction of the hotel's collection of historical photographs. Also ask whether you can visit the art deco Redwood Room—paneled with the wood of a single 2,000-year-old redwood tree—to have a look at the stunning re-productions of some of Gustave Klimt's work. This has to be one of the most beautiful public piano bar/dining rooms you'll see in the city of San Francisco.

Although this beautiful hotel has played host to many celebrities and literary figures throughout history, one of the most notable is Sir Arthur Conan Doyle, creator of Sherlock Holmes, who spent some time here during a lecture tour in 1923.

Head back to the corner of Geary and Taylor Streets and go right to 501 Taylor Street, the:

4. **Birthplace of Isadora Duncan.** Duncan (1878–1927) was one of the most celebrated and innovative dancers of the early 20th century, and her origins here are noted by a plaque near the entrance to no. 501. While in residence here Isadora's parents divorced, leaving her mother and the children with little money, so the precocious Isadora in her teens—and her older sister, Elizabeth, opened a dance school in San Francisco. Duncan, who had quit school at the age of 10 to study dance, and her sister were eager to begin teaching their "new system," which was based on natural and improvisational movements that attempted to interpret music and poetry.

Isadora soon grew tired of teaching and was able to convince her mother to take her on tour with the little money they had managed to save. Sadly, Duncan's first dance recitals in this country were not well received. But when she took her modern, free-spirited, free-form dance to London, she was "discovered" by Mrs. Patrick Campbell, who introduced Duncan to high-society London, as well as British royalty. It wasn't long before Duncan was adored all over Europe, known as the first woman to dance barefoot on stage. She was also the first person to perform interpretive dance to the music of the great composers.

Duncan died in 1927 in Nice in a freak accident—her long red scarf (for which she had become famous) became

Union Square

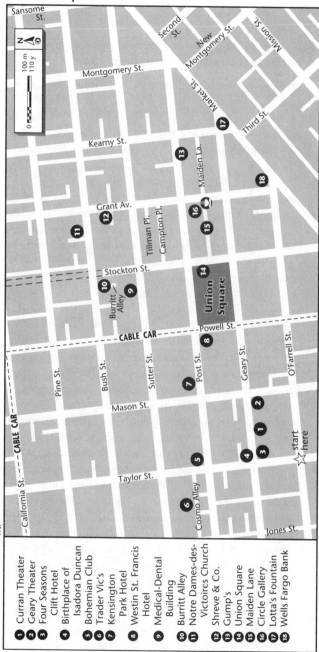

100 m
110 y

Sansome St.

Montgomery St.

Second St.

New Montgomery St.

Mission St.

Market St.

Third St.

Kearny St.

Maiden La.

Grant Av.

Tillman Pl.

Campton Pl.

Stockton St.

Burritt Alley

Union Square

Powell St.

CABLE CAR

Geary St.

Sutter St.

Post St.

O'Farrell St.

Pine St.

Bush St.

Mason St.

CABLE CAR

California St.

Taylor St.

Cosmo Alley

Jones St.

start here

9737

1 Curran Theater
2 Geary Theater
3 Four Seasons Clift Hotel
4 Birthplace of Isadora Duncan
5 Bohemian Club
6 Trader Vic's
7 Kensington Park Hotel
8 Westin St. Francis Hotel
9 Medical-Dental Building
10 Burritt Alley
11 Notre Dames-des-Victoires Church
12 Shreve & Co.
13 Gump's
14 Union Square
15 Maiden Lane
16 Circle Gallery
17 Lotta's Fountain
18 Wells Fargo Bank

entangled in the wheel of her Bughatti sports car, and she was strangled to death.

Continue along Taylor Street to the corner of Post Street where you'll find the ivy-covered, very exclusive:

5. **Bohemian Club.** You might be inclined to walk right by because, in spite of its size and relative bulk, the Bohemian Club is rather unobtrusive. You won't find much in the way of a sign either. The building you see today is a replacement for the original, which was destroyed in the 1906 earthquake.

Begun in 1872, the Bohemian Club grew out of a breakfast club for newspapermen that was first organized by James Bowan, a writer for the *San Francisco Chronicle.* Later other newspapermen and some artists and writers were granted membership. Some of the Bohemian Club's first members—true bohemians—included Ambrose Bierce, John Muir, Bret Harte, and George Sterling. The latter is often referred to as King of Bohemia, or the Last Bohemian.

Sterling was a serious and prolific poet. In his life he wrote 18 volumes of poetry, 13 of them published by Harry Robertson of San Francisco. Among the more notable were *Wine of Wizardry, The Testimony of the Suns,* and *Lilith.* Many individual poems were republished in eastern magazines, and Harper & Row brought out a short volume in 1925. Sterling, who had begun his career under the direction of his mentor, Ambrose Bierce, was granted membership to the club in 1904 but didn't take living quarters here until the 1920s. Sterling met his most unfortunate end in 1926 when he was awaiting the arrival of H. L. Mencken, for whom he had made elaborate arrangements in the way of dinners and parties. Mencken, oblivious to Sterling's plans and perhaps even to Sterling himself, decided to stay over in Los Angeles for a few more days. Sterling was so upset that he drank himself into a stupor; when Mencken finally did arrive, Sterling was too drunk to greet him. Nor was Sterling able to play his role as master of ceremonies in the festivities in Mencken's honor that evening; he was promptly replaced. So devastated was Sterling by this social failure that he proceeded to consume a lethal dose of cyanide, right here in his room at the Bohemian Club.

Today the club has strayed far from its original bohemian roots. It's an exclusive gentleman's club whose members are doctors, lawyers, and wealthy businessmen.

Few women have ever been allowed to enter the Bohemian Club, but one of those women was Ina Donna Coolbrith. A great friend of Mark Twain and Bret Harte, Coolbrith is one of four women who have been honored with an associate membership in the club.

Note the Bohemian Club plaque on the Taylor Street side of the corner. It features the Bohemian Club owl and the motto "Weaving Spiders Come Not Here." Go around the corner on Post Street and you'll find a fine bronze bas-relief of Bret Harte characters by Jo Mora (1919). The interior of the club also has an extraordinary collection of art, but since the club is private, you won't be able to go in and take a look.

Across Taylor Street from the Bohemian Club, in Cosmo Alley, is the original:

6. **Trader Vic's.** Now an international chain, the first restaurant opened under the direction of Vic Bergeron, and this one is still run by members of his family.

A literary group meets monthly in the Captain's Cabin (a rather unattractive room) at the Captain's Table. The group is very exclusive, and it is said that if a member of this roundtable fails to attend meetings for several months in a row, his champagne glass is dashed to smithereens (with decorum and ceremony, of course), and sent to him.

Come back out of Cosmo Alley the way you came in and go left on Taylor to Sutter Street. Go right onto Sutter. If you like, drop in at the Academy of Arts College Gallery, where you might even see the work of some great, not-yet-discovered artist. Just beyond the Academy of Arts College Gallery is a fun and whimsical shop called Robert Kuhn Antiques.

Continue along Sutter Street to Mason Street, where you will turn right. Walk one block to Post Street and turn left. You'll come to a shop called La Parisienne at 460 Post Street (on your left), which has interesting posters, costume jewelry, gifts, and hats that come all the way from Paris. If you continue along you'll find yourself right in front of the:

Ambrose Gwinett Bierce

Ambrose Bierce (1842–1914?) was born in Ohio, and after serving in the Civil War, he embarked on a career in journalism. When he came to San Francisco he began as a writer for the *News Letter*, becoming its editor in 1868.

He was lured to England to write for a London newspaper and was very successful there, but the climate aggravated his asthma so he returned to San Francisco to work for the *San Francisco Examiner*. Gertrude Atherton described his column "Prattle" in the *Sunday Examiner* as "brilliant, scarifying, witty, bitter, humorous and utterly fearless." Each week he skewered the famous and eminent so that "we were always expecting to hear that he had been shot." In 1896 he went to Washington as an *Examiner* correspondent to fight against the Funding Bill of the Central Pacific Railroad. He remained until 1913, writing for various publications, when he left suddenly for Mexico and was never seen again. Besides his journalism, Bierce wrote tales of horror, poetry, and other prose works. Perhaps his two most well-known collections are *Tales of Soldiers and Civilians* (1891) and *Can Such Things Be?* (1893). Today, he is probably most remembered for *The Devil's Dictionary* (1911), which was originally published as *The Cynic's Word Book* in 1906.

7. **Kensington Park Hotel.** Formerly the home of the local Elks Club, this building now houses the Theater on the Square as well as the Kensington. Go into the lobby and you'll find an old advertisement over the fireplace that boasts 100 rooms with a tub or shower for $2.50 to $3.50. The theater's entrance is on the second floor. Do go in and have a look around—there are some beautifully carved woodwork and balconies, as well as some lovely old chandeliers.

Exit left out of the hotel and continue along Post Street to the corner of Powell Street. On your right you'll see the:

8. **Westin St. Francis Hotel,** built in 1904 for Charles T. Crocker, who recognized San Francisco's need for a higher

class hotel to accommodate the upscale needs of the Bonanza Kings. Crocker used the latest technology in his plans for the hotel, even installing a system of pipes that were able to carry water directly from the ocean into the hotel's Turkish baths. Some even say that the St. Francis was the first hotel to use sheets on its beds.

The hotel, like most San Francisco buildings, was badly damaged during the earthquake and fire of 1906 and had to be rebuilt. Not long after its reconstruction, the hotel was further expanded, becoming the largest hotel on the West Coast.

Today, I'd recommend a trip inside just to see the enormous lobby and its huge shopping arcade (you'll see some pretty expensive items in the display cases—just in case you forgot your triple strand of pearls with the aquamarine diamond clasp). There are seven restaurants in the hotel, and glass elevators ride up the Union Square side of the building.

The Hotel St. Francis has some legendary history too. In 1921 the death here of Virginia Rappe began the Fatty Arbuckle scandal, which ended his career. Dashiell Hammett, while working for Pinkerton, was seen gathering evidence for Arbuckle's counsel right here in the lobby. It is also where Gerald Ford escaped assassin Sara Jane Moore's bullet in 1975.

Exit the hotel the same way you entered and head up Powell Street (going left if you're facing Union Square on Post Street) to Sutter Street. Go right on Sutter to the:

9. **Medical-Dental Building** at No. 450, designed by Timothy Pflueger and built in 1929. Go inside and view the handsome art deco interior. You'll best be able to see the Mayan art deco design by looking up at the cast-aluminum ceiling.

Also here in the building, to the left of the entrance, is a delightful Japanese art gallery, Kabutoya Galleries, which displays an interesting collection of modern Japanese prints (they're reasonably priced as well). Across the lobby, the Glass Pheasant specializes in glass pieces such as figurines, paper-weights, and vases, including Lalique.

Continue along Sutter Street to Stockton Street. Go left up Stockton and go up the stairs to Bush Street. Go left on Bush to:

10. **Burritt Alley.** If you're a Dashiell Hammett fan, you'll know this infamous spot where Hammett's fictional character Miles Archer (Sam Spade's sidekick) was shot. Head into the alley where you'll find a plaque commemorating the event. It says (in typical Hammett-ese), "On approximately this spot Miles Archer, partner of Sam Spade, was done in by Brigid O'Shaughnessy."

Directly across Bush Street from Burritt Alley at No. 608 you'll find a plaque remembering Robert Louis Stevenson, who lodged here living on 45 cents a day in 1879. He had come to San Francisco to be near Fanny Osbourne,who would later become his wife. The unknown, sick, and jobless writer was described by his landlady, Mrs. Carson, as "such a strange looking shabby shock of a fellow."

Note: If you were to walk a bit farther down Bush Street, past Burritt Alley toward Powell Street, you'd come to Dashiell Hammett Street.

Backtrack along Bush Street to Stockton Street, and continue on to 564 Bush Street, where you'll find:

12. **Notre Dames-des-Victoires Church.** Built in 1913, this church is difficult to miss because its architecture is so dramatically different from that of its modern neighbor. The present structure was built on the site of San Francisco's first French church. If you go inside you'll find photographs of what the area looked like after the earthquake of 1989.

Exit the church and go left on Bush Street to Grant Avenue. Go right on Grant. After you cross Sutter Street, you will come to Tillman Place, a short street on your right. Head into Tillman Place where you'll find the Tillman Place Bookshop. It might be small, but this little bookstore is just jam-packed with fascinating titles, including a great selection of travel books.

As you continue on Grant you'll also find several galleries, including the Erika Meyerovich Gallery at 231 Grant

Avenue (on your right), and the John Berggruen Gallery at 228 Grant Avenue (on your left). Both galleries house contemporary exhibits and are definitely worth stopping into if you're an art lover—there are some astonishing pieces here.

12. **Shreves & Co.,** a jeweler and the oldest retailer in the city. Shreves moved to this location just before the 1906 earthquake. Fortunately, it was one of the buildings left standing here when the dust cleared. It's worth looking in the cases even if you can't afford the contents.

Go left on Post and you will come to San Francisco's most famous department store,

13. **Gump's,** at 135 Post Street. Gump's recently moved from its previous location at 350 Post Street, where it had been for over 100 years, to this new address.

If you're looking for a toilet seat cover and a bath mat, I'd advise you to look elsewhere, because Gump's isn't your average everyday department store. This place is special.

Inside you'll find Gump's paperweight collection, as well as a wonderful display of Gump's San Francisco Porcelains—beautifully detailed miniatures of San Francisco Victorians (Painted Ladies), as well as a spectacular collection of Asian art.

In the museum tradition, Gump's will often display special items—an inlay table, for instance, along with a book on the art of inlay so that you can read more about the different types of inlay and how such treasures are created. Everything in the store is in its own way a work of art (a condition duly reflected in the prices of the items on sale).

The department store also has its own art gallery, which displays contemporary works. In the past, Gump's also hosted a collector lecture series throughout the year.

Going into Gump's is a pleasurable experience. Everything is so beautifully and artfully displayed that you won't mind the crowds because there are so many wonderful things to see. Even if you're one of those people who hates department stores, you couldn't possibly hate Gump's.

When you tire of looking at the treasures here and wish to move on, go left on Post upon exiting the store. As you walk back toward Grant Avenue and Stockton Street, you'll pass the flagship Williams Sonoma store at 150 Post Street. Inside, on the wall on the landing between the two floors, is an interesting collection of antique pastry implements.

Continue along Post Street to the corner of Stockton Street. To your left and ahead is:

14. **Union Square,** so-named because it was here that meetings were held in support of the Union side during the Civil War. The square has always been a gathering place for the citizens of San Francisco. In the 1960s it's where the flower children came hoping to enlighten people and gather new members for their counterculture. It is also where a gay activist group, the Sisters of Perpetual Indulgence, organized in 1987 to protest the visit of Pope John Paul II by seeking to have Harvey Milk canonized.

The Gump Brothers

The Gump brothers, Solomon and Gustave, arrived in San Francisco from Germany in 1850, hoping, like everyone else who was heading west, to strike it rich. They opened a frame and mirror shop, which did well because there were many newly wealthy people in the city who were looking to decorate their homes. Later, Solomon began traveling the world looking for merchandise. Each time he returned he brought back statuettes, paintings, sculptures, and porcelains for his own personal collection. His house became so full of these treasures that he was forced to take them to the shop and sell them. The Gumps' department store opened in 1861.

After 1900, Abraham Livingston Gump, who was nearly blind, took over the family business. It is he who is credited with having established Gump's as the leading dealer in Asian arts and antiquities on the West Coast.

Today, artists sometimes display their work (some is pretty good) and people mill around or just sit on the benches enjoying the sunshine or a quick lunch. You will also notice that the square is a favorite napping place for a portion of the city's homeless population. The center of San Francisco's most chic shopping district, the square is surrounded by Louis Vuitton, Saks Fifth Avenue, Macy's, and Hermès, just to name a few.

As you head up the palm-lined steps (the palm trees were planted here by John McLaren, caretaker of Golden Gate Park) to the center of the square, you'll see a 90-foot granite shaft with a bronze statue of Victory at the top. The model for the statue was the famous San Franciscan socialite Mrs. Adolph de Bretteville Spreckels. It was erected in celebration of Admiral Dewey's victory at Manila Bay during the Spanish-American War and was dedicated by Theodore Roosevelt in 1903. Amazingly enough, it did not fall during the earthquake in 1906.

You might also be interested to know that every summer the Cable Car Bell Ringing Competition is held here.

After you've finished exploring the square and browsing the high-priced boutiques and department stores that surround it, head across Stockton Street into:

15. **Maiden Lane,** a pedestrian street named by local jeweler Alfred Samuels. There is some speculation that he named it after the famous Maiden Lane in Manhattan, but no one is exactly sure. It was known as Morton Alley before 1906, then lined with many of the city's low-class brothels. Morton Alley was home to much debauchery, and it is said that there were about two murders a week on this street alone. In 1906 the street and surrounding area burned, forcing the prostitutes out of their storefronts where, as in Amsterdam's Red Light District, they had customarily posed in the windows plying their trade. City officials and residents vowed to keep the area clean and safe, so the street name was changed to Maiden Lane, and the prostitutes were no longer allowed.

As you walk along Maiden Lane you'll come to 140 Maiden Lane, on your left, the:

16. **Circle Gallery.** Designed in 1949 by Frank Lloyd Wright, this building is considered by many to be the precursor to the architect's design for the Guggenheim Museum in New York. It features a similar "snail-like" spiral design, except on a smaller scale. It is also the only Frank Lloyd Wright building in San Francisco.

    You can go in the gallery and walk up the spiral ramp, viewing contemporary works that are for sale here. This isn't a museum, so there's no admission fee. Go on in and have a look. And, just like at the Guggenheim, you'll have the opportunity to admire the architecture as well as the art on display.

    Take a Break Continue along Maiden Lane and you'll come to **Mocca** (175 Maiden Lane), a nice place to stop for a cold drink, a sandwich, salad, whole lunch platters, or just some appetizers. In warm weather diners may enjoy their meals al fresco. Mocca is open Monday through Saturday for breakfast and lunch.

    Follow Maiden Lane across Grant Avenue and continue along, passing Orientations, an Asian art shop. At the end of Maiden Lane, go right on Kerney Street to Market Street, where you'll find:

17. **Lotta's Fountain,** which is difficult to miss since it sits at the very busy intersection of Geary, Kearny, and Market streets. The fountain is named for Lotta Crabtree, who is said to have been one of the first children to have arrived in San Francisco.

    Lotta's mother brought her daughter with her to San Francisco when she came in search of her husband, who had sent them word that he was in California but declined to say exactly where in California. The city was made up mostly of men at that time, and the roughneck miners had never seen such a beautiful child or heard such an infectious laugh. Legend has it that they paraded her around on their shoulders. It didn't take long for Lotta's mother to grow tired of waiting for her husband to reappear, so she searched around for ways to make money. She soon realized that Lotta had natural beauty and a talent for entertaining and began to allow her daughter to perform in front of audiences. Those same men who once tenderly carried Lotta on their shoulders flocked to see her dance. Realizing the profitability of her daughter's gifts, Mrs. Crabtree took Lotta on tour with much success. After many years of touring, Lotta became the best-known and best-paid actress of her generation (she stopped touring in 1891).

The fountain you see today was donated by Lotta Crabtree to the city of San Francisco, but over the years it has been downsized a bit (the water troughs have been removed, and eight feet taken off the top of the main shaft). The fountain is both loved and loathed by San Franciscans. You'll have to admit that it is pretty ugly, but it is its ugliness that has made it one of San Francisco's most famous landmarks.

So famous, in fact, that Luisa Tetrazzini, one of San Francisco's best-loved opera singers, sang a Christmas Eve performance right here at Lotta's Fountain.

Look to your left on Market Street and you'll see the Hearst Building at 691–699 Market Street. It is just one of three newspaper buildings that used to be on this street.

Luisa Tetrazzini

Luisa Tetrazzini (1871–1940), an Italian opera soprano, made her debut in Florence in 1895, and soon after she performed in Spain, Portugal, Russia, and Latin America. In 1904 she made her debut in San Francisco—she fell in love with the city and its people, and the city fell in love with her.

Tetrazzini left San Francisco to sing in New York, under contract with Oscar Hammerstein. Hammerstein and Tetrazzini, both hot-tempered artists, were soon at each other's throats when Tetrazzini wanted to return to San Francisco. She told newspaper reporters, "I will sing in San Francisco, for I know the streets of San Francisco are free." She and Hammerstein became embroiled in a legal battle which Tetrazzini eventually won. It was upon her return the following Christmas Eve that she made her appearance at Lotta's Fountain.

Go right on Market Street. The Beaux-Arts building on your right at number 744 Market Street is the:

18. **Wells Fargo Bank.** If you wish, you can also visit the Wells Fargo Museum in the bank's branch at 420 Montgomery Street, between California and Sacramento streets, during banking hours; the museum houses artifacts from early San Francisco, including a stagecoach, a collection of mail, and a panorama of San Francisco in 1863.

If you look directly ahead from the bank (looking up Market Street) you'll see the Phelan Building, a classic example of flat-iron architecture. Here you get a fantastic view of the structure, which stretches on for blocks and comes together in a point directly in front of you.

Also ahead of you, on a diagonal to your left, is another architecturally compelling structure, only this time it's modern. The Marriott Hotel was designed in 1989 by architect Anthony Lumsden, and it's another building (like the Transamerica Pyramid) that many San Franciscans both love and loathe which probably assures its place in San Francisco's colorful architectural history. It is particularly stunning at sunset with the shimmering reflections of sunlight on its facade.

From the Wells Fargo Bank you can continue along Market Street to Hallidie Plaza at the corner of Powell and Market streets, where you'll find the San Francisco Convention and Visitor's Bureau (down a flight of stairs). You can also get BART or the Muni here.

CHINATOWN

Start: Corner of Grant Avenue and Bush Street.

Public Transportation: 9X or 15 bus to Bush and Kearny streets.

Finish: Corner of Ross Alley and Jackson Street.

Time: 2 hours, not including museum or shopping stops.

Best Times: Every day from 11am to 9pm when there's the most action.

Worst Times: Too early or too late because shops will be closed and no one will be milling around.

Hills That Could Kill: None.

When the first Chinese immigrants came to San Francisco they found a very small town centered on Portsmouth Plaza (now Portsmouth Square). Like everyone else, they began settling around the town square, but it wasn't until the gold rush that the Chinese came in droves to the United States, where they were exploited as cheap labor. Most of the immigrants were men. Fleeing famine and the Opium Wars, they had nothing to lose and everything to gain by coming to the "Golden Mountain" of California.

By 1850 the Chinese community had grown to over 4,000. The community was primarily male and was organized by clans, each of which operated different types of businesses. For example, the Sanyi controlled the companies that were successful outside the Chinese community, like import/export businesses. Another clan, from the Nanhai District, were primarily manufacturers of men's clothing; they also ran butcher shops. Families from the Shunde District mass-produced workmen's clothing. Another group controlled the fish industry, while yet another made women's clothing and undergarments. The group with the smallest amount of economic power was also the largest, and they ran the restaurants and laundries. These were their "involuntary associations."

The tongs, on the other hand, were "voluntary associations." There were tongs whose purpose was to protect the community, and there were tongs whose purpose was to rob the community. The latter were the most profitable, and controlled prostitution, opium smuggling, loan-sharking, and gambling. Like all gangs, tongs often engaged in turf wars. The most notorious leader to rise out of these wars was "Little Pete," a gambler and racketeer who adopted Western dress, cut off his traditional queue (the pigtail traditionally worn by Chinese men), and hired a white bodyguard. He was hated in Chinatown and was killed as he sat in a barber's chair waiting to be shaved.

The Chinese were cut off from the rest of the population and persecuted, robbed, beaten, and murdered with impunity. Chinese laundries and restaurants were set on fire; one of the favorite pastimes of young hoodlums was to tie a Chinese man's queue to the bars of the cable cars so that they would be dragged along when they tried to disembark. Anti-Chinese sentiment grew in the late 1850s when the city's prosperity ebbed, increasing further in the 1870s when many more Chinese entered the country to work building the Southern Pacific Railroad.

The persecution reached a crest in 1874 when a set of resolutions against the Chinese was passed at a mass meeting of San Francisco residents and sent to President Grant. A more violent event occurred in 1877 when the Sand-Lot Orator, Dennis Kearny, raised the cry "The Chinese *must* go!" inciting a backlash against the Chinese, who were pelted with bricks and forced to watch as their properties and businesses were smashed. Anti-Chinese feeling ultimately led to the passage of the Chinese Exclusion Act in 1882, which effectively stopped Chinese immigration; it is estimated that the Chinese population of

San Francisco at that time was approximately 50,000. Later, as fewer Chinese immigrants came to San Francisco, and after the revolution in China in 1911, the Chinese who were in California started to shed their clannishness and cultural isolation and began to assimilate. They cut off their queues and began to adopt Western styles of dress.

In 1943, as a result of China's alliance with the United States during World War II, the Chinese Exclusion Act was repealed and a quota of 105 Chinese immigrants a year established.

This section of San Francisco is tiny and is bounded loosely by Broadway, Stockton, Kearny, and Bush streets. Nevertheless, it makes for a very interesting walk because this is the place where the tiny community of Yerba Buena first began. It's the place where the first tent was pitched and the first house was erected. There were many more firsts here in Chinatown, and you'll get to see where they're located or where they took place as you walk along this tour.

● ● ● ● ● ● ● ● ● ● ● ● ● ● ● ●

To begin, walk over to Grant Avenue from the bus stop at Bush and Kearny streets and head up Grant through the:

1. **Chinatown Gateway Arch.** It is traditional in China that villages have ceremonial gates like this one, which was donated by the Chinese Chamber of Commerce. This gate is a lot less formal than those in China, built here more for the benefit of the tourist industry than anything else. Note the Fu Dogs (which traditionally guard Chinese temples) on either side and the dragons on top.

Go right at the corner of Pine Street, crossing to the left side of Pine, and on your left you'll come to:

2. **St. Mary's Square,** where you'll find a huge metal and granite statue of Dr. Sun Yat-sen, the founder of the Republic of China. A native of Guandong (Canton) Province, Sun Yat-sen's goal was to overthrow the Qing Dynasty, and he traveled all around the world in an effort to raise money for the intended revolution. While he lived in San Francisco, Sun founded a newspaper in the Montgomery Block. (For more information about the Montgomery Block, see Walking Tour 3, stop 2.)

The notable feature about the statue, which was sculpted by Benjamino Bufano, is the figure's shining stainless steel cloak. Sun Yat-sen, "Champion of Democracy" and "Proponent of Peace and Friendship among Nations," as the statue's pedestal proclaims, looks out over the benches and playground here and sometimes reflects a beautiful sunset in his "silver" cloak.

Cross to the other side of the square toward California Street, and you'll see the clock across the street that warns, "Son, observe the time and fly from evil." You'll be standing in front of:

3. **Old St. Mary's Church.** The first cathedral in San Francisco, St. Mary's was built primarily by Chinese laborers and dedicated on Christmas Day, 1854. The Chinese call the church Dai Choong Low, or "Tower of the Big Bell." Because it was built of brick (which was transported around Cape Horn) and granite (which came all the way from China), it was one of the lucky survivors of the 1906 earthquake and later weathered the quake of 1989 as well. The church was also the site of the community's first English-language school. Visiting is allowed, but the church isn't always open.

Continue left past the church on California Street, and when you get to Grant Avenue again, go right. Here you'll find a shop called the:

4. **Canton Bazaar,** at 616 Grant Avenue. You can buy all kinds of Chinese wares here, including porcelain, antiques, glassware, embroideries, and cloisonné. Some of the merchandise is rather tacky, but if you've got a good eye you should be able to sort through and find a souvenir or two. There's even some nice carved and rattan furniture here.

Continue up Grant Avenue, and as you approach Sacramento Street, note on your right at the southeast corner of Sacramento Street and Grant Avenue the:

5. **Bank of America,** which is in the traditional Chinese architectural style. There are dragons all over this building—on the front doors and encircling the columns. All told, there are approximately 60 dragon medallions on this facade.

Chinatown

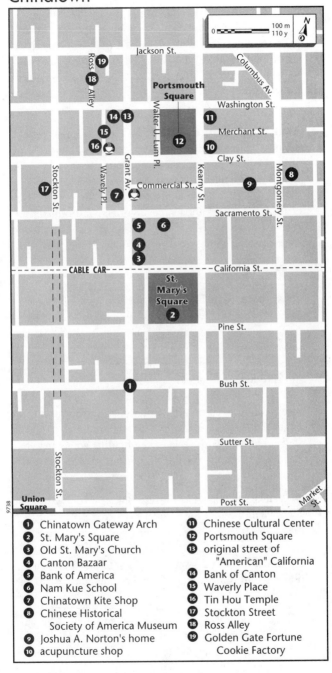

1. Chinatown Gateway Arch
2. St. Mary's Square
3. Old St. Mary's Church
4. Canton Bazaar
5. Bank of America
6. Nam Kue School
7. Chinatown Kite Shop
8. Chinese Historical Society of America Museum
9. Joshua A. Norton's home
10. acupuncture shop
11. Chinese Cultural Center
12. Portsmouth Square
13. original street of "American" California
14. Bank of Canton
15. Waverly Place
16. Tin Hou Temple
17. Stockton Street
18. Ross Alley
19. Golden Gate Fortune Cookie Factory

An interesting side note: This is just a small branch of a bank originally created by A. P. Giannini (an Italian American born in San Jose) and known as the Bank of Italy (later the Bank of America). He wanted to help immigrants who didn't have much money and couldn't get help from other, bigger banks.

Go right on Sacramento Street until you come to the:

6. **Nam Kue School at No. 755.** This is a school where Chinese American children go for a couple of hours in the afternoon after American school to learn about their traditions, culture, and the Cantonese language.

A little farther along on the left is the Chinese Chamber of Commerce at 730 Sacramento Street. You can stop in here for more specialized information about different resources, shops, and services in Chinatown Monday through Friday during business hours.

Return to Grant Avenue and go right to the:

7. **Chinatown Kite Shop,** on your left at 717 Grant Avenue. You'll find a wonderful assortment of Chinese kites here. Some are hand painted, some are simply decorative (like windsocks), and some are sturdy stunt kites. The Chinese use kites as a great form of entertainment. They take specially designed stunt kites, climb up on the roofs of their houses, and launch into kite fights with their neighbors. Kite fighting is taken very seriously as a sport, and as a result, the stakes can often be very high.

Though you won't see any kite-fighting going on here, you might be able to find some great, easy-to-transport souvenirs.

Take a Break   The **Eastern Bakery** is located at 720 Grant Avenue, on the right-hand corner of Grant and the narrow Commercial Street. First opened in 1924, Eastern Bakery is the oldest Chinese American bakery in San Francisco. If you really want to give your palate an education, try some mooncakes, almond cookies, lotus cakes, or sweet bow ties here.

When you feel that sugar surge, head up just a bit farther along Grant Avenue. You'll come across the Wok Shop at 804 Grant Avenue, where you can purchase just about any utensil, cookbook, or vessel you might need to do Chinese style cooking in your own kitchen.

When you come out of the Wok Shop, go left; when you get back to Commercial Street go left again. Continue on past Kearny Street and Montgomery Street, and at No. 650 Commercial Street, on your left, you'll see the:

8. **Chinese Historical Society of America Museum,** founded in 1963. It boasts that it is the first Chinese American organization to have had a U.S. president as an honorary member (Lyndon B. Johnson). The museum's small but fascinating collection tells much about the role of Chinese immigrants in American history, particularly in San Francisco and the rest of California. The goals of the museum are to "study, record, acquire, and preserve all suitable artifacts and such cultural items as manuscripts, books, and works of art . . . which have a bearing on the history of the Chinese living in the United States of America, and to promote the contributions that Chinese Americans living in this country have made to the United States of America." Some of the most interesting artifacts on display include a papier-mâché dragon's head mask dating from 1909, a shrimp cleaning machine, 19th-century clothing and slippers of the Chinese pioneers, Chinese herbs and scales, some historic hand-carved and painted shop signs, and a series of photographs that document the development of Chinese culture in America.

Admission is free, but the museum appreciates any donation you can give. It's open from about noon to 4pm Tuesday through Saturday. The curator sometimes closes early if there are no visitors, so get there well before 4pm if you want to visit.

Exit the museum and go right, toward Kearny Street. As you walk, note that Commercial Street in the block between Montgomery and Kearny streets was:

9. **Joshua A. Norton's home.** Norton, the self-proclaimed "Emperor of the United States and Protector of Mexico," used to walk around the streets in an old, brass-buttoned military uniform, sporting a hat with a "dusty plume." He lived in a fantasy world, and San Franciscans humored him at every turn.

Norton was born around 1815 in the British Isles and sailed as a young man to South Africa, where he served as a colonial rifleman. He came to San Francisco in 1849 with $40,000 and proceeded to double and triple his fortune in real estate. Unfortunately for him, he next chose to go into the rice business. While Norton was busy cornering the market and forcing prices up, several ships loaded with rice arrived unexpectedly in San Francisco harbor. The rice market was suddenly flooded, and Norton was forced into bankruptcy. He left San Francisco for about three years and must have experienced a breakdown of some sort, for upon his return, Norton thought he was an emperor.

Instead of ostracizing him, San Franciscans embraced him as their own home-grown lunatic. He was given free meals all over town. Gertrude Atherton said that "he walked majestically into banks, stores, and mercantile houses and presented formal bills for taxes. The sums were small and were paid with good-natured humor. They were acknowledged by a formal receipt, decorated with a great seal, and inscribed, 'Norton I, Emperor of the U.S.A.' The City Council voted him one of the expenses of the city treasury."

In addition, Norton I issued hundreds of proclamations and governmental decrees which were "composed in superior English, in which he expressed his displeasure over political conditions, and about war and peace and municipal affairs." He would also issue commands to other world leaders, thinking nothing about sending orders directly to General Grant. His proclamations were always printed in the newspaper without complaint, and San Franciscans of all ages read them with interest. Some of them even sent him fake telegrams from the Prime Minister of England and the President of Mexico.

When Emperor Norton died in 1880, 10,000 people passed by his coffin, which was bought with money raised at the Pacific Union Club, and over 30,000 people participated in the funeral procession.

When you get to Kearny Street, notice that on the corner are the offices of the *Sing Tao Daily*. Go right on Kearny, passing an:

10. **acupuncture shop** at 704 Kearny Street. It's fun to go inside these places, which are sprinkled throughout Chinatown, and explore the different kinds of medicinal roots, herbs, and teas that are sold here. You'll likely see someone who is waiting for his or her dose of needle therapy.

A bit farther up Kearny Street is the:

11. **Chinese Cultural Center,** in the Holiday Inn at No. 750, at the corner of Merchant Street. On your way into the building, take a look at the plaque on your left as you head up the stairs to the front door. Its inscription commemorates the fact that this was the site of the old Jenny Lind Theatre in 1851.

The theater was opened in October of 1850 by Tom Maguire over his Parker House saloon and gambling hall, which was located on this very spot. Although Maguire didn't know Jenny Lind, nor did she ever sing here, he did admire her. So that's why the theater bore her name. Unfortunately, Maguire's gambling hall burned down in May of 1851. Maguire persevered and built another theater, but just nine days later that one burned too. Frustrated but bull-headed, Tom Maguire built a third (of stone this time) which opened on October 4, 1851. Two years later his luck ran out—he went bankrupt and had to sell the building to the city. It was then used as City Hall.

Go in and take the elevator up to the Chinese Cultural Center on the third floor. The center is oriented more to the community than to tourists, offering lectures, films, and seminars to members; however, as a tourist, you might be interested in their rotating exhibits of Asian art and writing. If you find that you're developing more than a passing interest in the art of Chinese cooking, you can make arrangements to go on a culinary walking tour. The guide will take you to various Chinese groceries, naming and explaining the uses of the many unfamiliar Chinese herbs, spices, and vegetables, and other staples of the Chinese kitchen. The tour, which includes lunch, requires advance reservations.

Come out of the Chinese Cultural Center and take the pedestrian walkway leading from the third floor of the Holiday Inn over Kearny Street to:

12. **Portsmouth Square,** the very center of San Francisco's Chinese community. It was also once the center of Yerba Buena, and though it's difficult to imagine now, the plaza was right at the water's edge. At that time it was used by villagers to corral their animals. In 1846, when Americans first came to California and claimed it as American territory, the marines who landed named the square after their ship, the USS *Portsmouth*.

It was also in Portsmouth Square on March 29, 1849, that Sam Brannan (who arrived on the USS *Brooklyn* shortly after the USS *Portsmouth*) helped to start the gold rush by running through the plaza waving a glass jar "filled with some glittering substance," yelling, "Gold! Gold, gold, gold from American River." It should be noted here that Brannan also ran a San Francisco newspaper, the *Califonia Star*, had ridiculed its rival, the *Californian,* when that paper first broke the story two weeks earlier (in a somewhat quieter manner).

Brannan did more than start the gold rush, he was also instrumental in starting the vigilante committees formed after a rash of fires (six of them) in 1851 burned the small city. The fires were arson, started by two groups of hooligans, the Hounds (from New York) and the Sydney Ducks (from Australia), who ran amok in the city, robbing, looting, and killing. Brannan finally reached a breaking point and called a meeting in Portsmouth Square to discuss actions that could be taken outside the law. In the end, the Hounds were run out of the city or captured fairly quickly and without bloodshed. The Ducks were a bit more difficult to convince.

The first official Vigilante Executive Committee was formed in 1851, vowing to perform "every lawful act for the maintenance of law and order," because they believed that no one's life or property was safe. The first man they arrested was a Sydney Duck by the name of Jenkins, who had been caught trying to steal a safe. The Commitee sentenced him to hang in Portsmouth Square, and he was executed there. Apparently the Sydney Ducks got the message because there were no more fires set during the two years the Vigilante Committee was active.

Today, the square serves more peaceful purposes. Some Chinatown residents practice tai chi here in the early morning. And throughout the day the square is heavily trafficked by children and—in large part—elderly men, who play cards and gamble with their friends.

A favorite spot of Rudyard Kipling, Jack London, and Robert Louis Stevenson, Portsmouth Square may once have been cleaner than it is today, but it was probably just as crowded. It is said that Robert Louis Stevenson used to love to sit on a bench here and watch life going on all around him. You'll find a monument to his memory at the northeast corner of the square, consisting of a model of the *Hispañola,* the ship in Stevenson's novel, *Treasure Island,* and an excerpt from his "Christmas Sermon." It says:

> *To be honest to be*
> *kind to earn a little*
> *to spend a little to*
> *make up on the whole a*
> *family happier for his*
> *presence to renounce when*
> *that shall be necessary*
> *and not be embittered*
> *to keep a few friends, but*
> *these without capitulation—*
> *above all on the same*
> *grim condition to keep*
> *friends with himself*
> *here is a task for*
> *all that a man has*
> *of fortitude and delicacy.*

Exit Portsmouth Square to the west and cross Walter U. Lum Place (the road in front of you). Go right to Washington Street, where you will turn left. As you cross Grant Avenue, note that you are standing at the head of the block that was the:

13. **Original street of "American" California.** At the end of the block, at the corner of Clay Street, the first tent was set up by an English seaman named William Richardson in 1835. A plaque between 823 and 837 Grant Avenue

commemorates this event. (If you decide to take a look, just backtrack to Washington Street and Grant Avenue and turn left.)

Look for 743 Washington Street, just across Grant Avenue, the:

14. **Bank of Canton,** located in the oldest Asian-style edifice in San Francisco—its Asian-style facade dates from 1909. This three-tiered temple-style building once housed the China Telephone Exchange. Known to Chinatown and San Francisco inhabitants as "China-5" until the mid-1940s, the exchange became famous for its operators, who knew by heart the phone numbers of all of Chinatown's inhabitants, and knew their habits so well that if a person were not at home, the operators were often able to track him or her down and get the call through anyway.

   Before that, this building was the 1848 home of San Francisco's first newspaper, Sam Brannan's *California Star,* which helped spread the news that gold had been discovered in the hills of California.

   Also here at the corner of Grant and Washington you'll see Chew Chong Tai & Co., the oldest store in Chinatown (c. 1910). Among other things, it's known for its fine assortment of Chinese and Japanese inks. Go left when you get to:

15. **Waverly Place,** or "The Street of Painted Balconies." This is probably Chinatown's most popular side street or alleyway because of its painted balconies and colorful architectural details. You can only admire the architecture from the ground because most of the buildings are private family associations or temples.

   One temple you can visit (but make sure it's open before you go climbing up the long narrow stairway) is the:

16. **Tin Hou Temple,** at 125 Waverly Place. Located on the fourth floor of this building, the Tin Hou Temple is dedicated to Tin Hou, the Queen of the Heavens and Goddess of the Seven Seas. Its color scheme is traditional, with black, red, and gold lacquered woods. There are some intricately carved wooden statues, and Chinese lanterns dangle from the ceilings. Take some time to meditate amid the flowers and aromas of burning incense.

Remember that you are welcome as a visitor, but you should respect those who are here to pray and try to be as unobtrusive as possible. It is customary to give a donation or buy a bundle of incense during your visit.

Note: If you couldn't get in to visit the temple on this trip, you can also visit on a guided tour arranged by the Chinese Culture Center (see stop 11 for details).

Take a Break Near the temple is **Pot Sticker,** also here at 150 Waverly Place. You might be hungry for lunch or a snack by now, and I'd recommend this place. As you might have guessed, the restaurant is named for its specialty—dumplings, fried or steamed (that often stick to the sides of the pot when cooked), stuffed with meats and/or vegetables. The place is a local favorite.

Keep traveling down Waverly Place, and go right when you get to Sacramento Street, then right again onto:

17. Stockton Street. From around Broadway to Sacramento Street, Stockton is where most of the residents of Chinatown do their daily shopping.

One interesting footnote to this block's history is a place called Cameron House (at the corner of Stockton and Sacramento streets), which was named for a woman by the name of Donaldina Cameron. Called Lo Mo, or "the Mother," by the Chinese, she spent her life trying to free Chinese women who had come to America in hopes of marrying well from an all-too-common fate—prostitution and slavery.

A good place to stop if you're in the market for some jewelry is Jade Galore at 1000 Stockton Street (at the corner of Stockton and Washington streets). In addition to purveying jade jewelry, they do a fair trade in diamonds here.

When you're finished at Jade Galore, you might like to keep wandering up Stockton Street absorbing the atmosphere and street life of this less tourist-oriented Chinese community before doubling back to Washington Street. Turn left, back toward Grant Avenue. About halfway along the block you'll see:

18. **Ross Alley** on your left. As you walk along Ross Alley, just one of the many alleyways that crisscrossed Chinatown to accommodate the many immigrants who jammed into the neighborhood, note on your left the sweatshops where women work as seamstresses. This is a section of Chinatown that is very reminiscent of Chinatown's not so pretty past.

As you approach the end of Ross Alley, note on your right the:

19. **Golden Gate Fortune Cookie Company,** at 56 Ross Street. The first time I saw this place I was simply astonished—I mean, when you hear the word "company," or "factory," you expect to see big machines and many people on an assembly line, right? Well, there's an assembly line here, but there are only two people on it. One sits in the chair closest to the door cutting up the strips of paper you and I know as the "fortune" in the fortune cookie. The other tends the machine that squirts small amounts of batter onto little circular presses that go around in a carousel-like fashion as they cook. The same woman removes each cooked, flattened cookie, places a fortune on it, and folds it into the traditional fortune cookie shape.

They'll let you watch for about five seconds before they pressure you to buy a bag. You can purchase regular fortunes or "sexy" ones (which are their specialty).

Exit the fortune cookie factory, turn right and go to the end of Ross Alley. You'll be at the corner of Jackson Street, where this tour ends. If you want, you can go back down Ross Alley, turn left on Washington Street, and before long arrive at the starting point for our next tour—North Beach.

North Beach

Start: Intersection of Montgomery Street, Columbus Avenue, and Washington Street.

Public Transportation: 41, 30X, or 15 bus as near as you can get to the intersection of Montgomery Street, Columbus Avenue, and Washington Street.

Finish: Washington Square.

Time: 3 hours, not including a stop for lunch.

Best Times: Start the tour Monday through Saturday at around 11am.

Worst Times: Sunday when shops are closed.

Hills That Could Kill: The Montgomery Street hill that runs from Broadway to Vallejo Street.

When most people think of North Beach they think Italian, but the Italians were actually the last group to arrive here. A group of Chilean prostitutes arrived first in the 1850s; they were followed by the Irish, who were later supplanted by a group of Latin Americans. The Italians didn't arrive until the late 1800s, and the Italian population didn't reach its peak until the turn of the century. In the 1950s North Beach became San Francisco's bohemian center, attracting beatniks and Beat poets such as Jack Kerouac, Lawrence Ferlinghetti, and Allen Ginsberg. Since the 1970s the Chinese community has been expanding out of Chinatown's traditional boundaries into North Beach, crossing Broadway, the unofficial border. In fact, although most shops and restaurants in the North Beach area are still Italian, the Chinese account for almost half of the neighborhood's population.

All this aside, North Beach remains the Italian center of San Francisco. You can get Italian food on practically every block, and chances are you'll see groups of men playing bocce ball in the park. You might even witness an Italian wedding at Saints Peter and Paul Church.

This tour will take you from Washington Street up through North Beach. In general, you'll be following Columbus Avenue and taking some detours to one side or the other. You will visit a small corner of San Francisco's original Financial District, including historic Jackson Square, before proceeding to many of the beatniks' favorite hangouts, including City Lights Bookstore. Finally, you'll end up in Washington Square, where you might be able to strike up a conversation with some elderly Italian men who remember North Beach in the early decades of this century. There's some great shopping here, and, of course, great food. Try to schedule your tour to include lunch or dinner.

● ● ● ● ● ● ● ● ● ● ● ● ● ● ● ●

After you get off the bus you can't help but notice the strange looking building on the corner, the:

1. **Transamerica Pyramid.** Noted for its spire (which rises 212 feet above the top floor) and its "wings" (which begin at the 29th floor and stop where the spire begins), the pyramid is San Francisco's tallest building and an identifying landmark of the city's skyline. It's also a good place to begin this tour—take the express elevator to the observation deck on the 27th floor (open weekdays only) and you'll be treated to a spectacular view of the city.

You may wish to take a peek at one of the rotating art exhibits in the lobby before getting on the elevator. When you reach the observation deck, you can use the map there to identify some of the landmarks you'll be visiting on this tour. For a small preview, note Coit Tower and Washington

North Beach

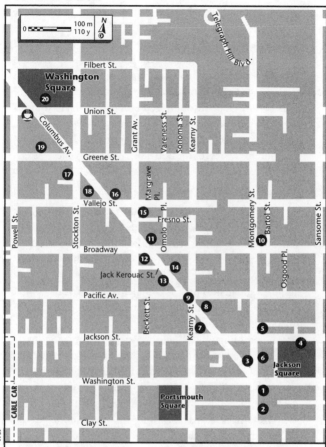

1. Transamerica Pyramid
2. The Montgomery Block
3. original Transamerica Building
4. 400 block of Jackson Square
5. William Stout Architecture Books
6. Golden Era Building
7. 599 Jackson Street
8. Purple Onion
9. Columbus Tower
10. 1010 Montgomery Street
11. Condor Club
12. City Lights Bookstore
13. Vesuvio Café
14. Spec's Adler Museum Café/Tosca Café
15. Caffe Trieste
16. Biordi Art Imports
17. North Beach Museum
18. R. Matteuchi Street Clock
19. Fugazi Hall
20. Washington Square

Square with its Saints Peter and Paul Catholic Church (more about these places later).

When you exit the Transamerica Pyramid, go around to the right and into the half-acre Redwood Park, which is part of the Transamerica Center. Year round you can sit here and enjoy the greenery, redwood trees, and the fountain. From May through September the Transamerica Corporation sponsors lunch time concerts here.

The site occupied by the Transamerica Pyramid, in addition to the rest of the 600 block of Montgomery Street, was once occupied by a historic building called:

2. **The Montgomery Block.** It was four stories high, and when it was built in 1853 it was the tallest building in the West. San Franciscans called it "Halleck's Folly" because it was built on a raft of redwood logs that had been bolted together and floated at the edge of the ocean (which was right at Montgomery Street at that time). It was a bit of architectural genius by Captain Henry Wager Halleck that in fact helped the building withstand several earthquakes, including the earthquake of 1906.

The building was demolished in 1959 but is fondly remembered for its historic importance as the power center of the city whose tenants also included artists and writers of all kinds, among them Jack London, George Sterling, Ambrose Bierce, Bret Harte, and Mark Twain. All of these men had offices in this block-long building and they would gather nearly every day at the marble-floored, mahogany Bank Exchange bar where beer was drawn from Wedgwood taps. The proprietor of the bar, a Scotsman named Duncan Nicol, invented the bar's famous drink, Pisco Punch (with a Peruvian brandy base), which was so strong that patrons were only allowed two glasses at a sitting. These literati also liked to hang out at Coppa's, which opened later and was located on the Merchant Street corner of the Montgomery Block. Coppa's is where bohemian San Francisco was born.

Sun Yat-sen's newspaper offices were here, as was George Sterling's office—on the fourth floor—where he would work on his verse in his robe every morning, and in which he hung approximately 20 portraits of himself. Other notable residents included Maynard Dixon, the muralist, and William Walker, the filibuster, who wrote his manifesto here.

William "Filibuster" Walker

The kind of filibustering referred to isn't the Congressional kind we hear so much about in the news. As used here, a filibuster is a person who engages in warfare, specifically fomenting insurrections, in countries with which his own country is at peace—a problem that reached a peak in the mid-nineteenth century when several Americans were fighting to control large parts of Latin America. Walker (1824–1860) was one of the most famous of these American filibusters. A doctor and lawyer at the age of 24, he still sought more power and began his filibustering in 1853. Acquitted by an American jury after attempting (and failing) to conquer southern California and the Sonora region of Mexico, Walker moved on to bigger things. In 1855 he set out to conquer Nicaragua, which he accomplished after capturing Granada in 1856. He declared himself president. With the help of Cornelius Vanderbilt (who originally backed Walker's venture), a Central American alliance defeated him the next year, and he was again brought back to the United States for trial. Again, he was acquitted. He made a final attempt to conquer all of Central America in 1860 but was held back by the British navy. Walker was executed in Honduras in September of that year. His book was called W*ar in Nicaragua* and was published in 1860.

Everybody who was anybody hung out here in the palm-dotted lobby. It was described by Idwal Jones, a Montgomery Block scholar, as the "social vortex of the city, of all of California" and the "meeting place of all professions." The offices were occupied by lawyers and judges, the shops leased to custom tailors, milliners, jewelers, and print sellers. Agoston Haraszthy, the founder of the California wine industry, leased space in the basement; and gold was refined, cast into ingots, and lowered into the vaults at Adams and Co. on the Merchant Street side. Everything, including banks, theaters, shops, and newspaper offices (if they weren't here), was within walking distance from the Montgomery Block.

The Montgomery Block was also the home of the *Daily Evening Bulletin* and the site of the James King William shooting (see "Introducing San Francisco" for more information about him).

From the southeast corner of Montgomery and Washington streets, look across Washington to the corner of Columbus Avenue, and you'll see the:

3. **original Transamerica Building,** across the street at 4 Columbus Avenue. A beaux arts flat-iron building covered in white terra-cotta, it was also the home of the old Fugazi Bank. Built for the Banco Populare Italiano Operaia Fugazi in 1909, it was originally a two-story building, but a third floor was added in 1916. In 1928, Fugazi merged his bank with the Bank of America, which was started by A. P. Giannini (see Walking Tour 2, stop 5 for details on this bank). Giannini also created the Transamerica Corporation, a holding company, which he headquartered here. The Transamerica Corporation remained here until 1972 when it moved into the Transamerica Pyramid across the street.

Go right on Montgomery Street and follow it to Sansome Street. Go left on Sansome to Jackson Street, where you should turn left. Now you're in the:

4. **400 block of Jackson Square,** where you'll find some of the only commercial buildings to survive the 1906 earthquake and fire. 415 Jackson served as the headquarters for the Ghirardelli chocolate company from 1855 to 1894 and was built around 1853. The Hotaling Building (No. 451) was built in 1866. At No. 472 is another of the buildings that survived the disaster of 1906.

You've probably already noticed that this is one of San Francisco's antique centers, but equally important, it is the architecture center. In addition to some of the most prestigious antique dealerships in town, you'll find several different architectural supply shops and architecture firms.

One of the greatest architecture bookstores around is:

5. **William Stout Architecture Books,** at 804 Montgomery Street (on the corner of Jackson and Montgomery

streets). It has an amazing collection of architecture books. If you happen to be looking for something that's a little esoteric, it's very likely that they'll have it here.

This incredible store evolved from a personal collection of only a few dozen books in William Stout's apartment to the current stock of (approximately) 11,000 hard-to-find books and magazines. William Stout is open every day except Sunday from 10am to 5:30pm. It's open later on Thursday evenings.

Go left when you come out of the bookstore, crossing Jackson Street, and follow Montgomery Street to No. 732, the:

6. **Golden Era Building,** on the left side of the street, erected in about 1852. The building is named after the literary magazine, the *Golden Era,* which was published here. Part of the group of young writers who worked on the magazine were known as the Bohemians, and they included Samuel Clemens (Mark Twain) and Bret Harte (who began as a typesetter here). Clemens and Harte were different in every way possible—Clemens was a sloppy dresser but a quick-witted writer; Harte was something of a dandy but suffered over every word he put on paper—yet they were the best of friends.

Continue down the block and stop for a minute to admire the annex, located at No. 728–30, of the building at No. 722. The Belli Annex, as it is currently known, is registered as a Historic Landmark. Built between 1853 and 1854 on the foundations of an 1849 building, this three-story Italianate brick structure was the original home of Freemasonry in California. A plaque tells us that it was here on October 17, 1849, that Lodge Number 1 had its first meeting.

Turn around and go back to Jackson Street. Go left on Jackson to the corner of Columbus Avenue (which was originally called Montgomery Avenue) where you'll find Thomas Brothers Maps at 550 Jackson Street, one of San Francisco's most comprehensive map stores. Continue towards Kearny Street and on the small triangular block between Kearny and Columbus is:

7. **599 Jackson Street,** the original location of a club called the "hungry i" (which is now located not far away on Broadway). A man by the name of "Big Daddy" Nordstrom was the owner of the first hungry i; he and his friend Mark Adams gave the club its name one day as they were driving around the city. Adams suggested the name "Hungry Id," for "the inner man's search." Big Daddy didn't like that name too much, so Adams shortened it to "hungry i," with lowercase letters, and Big Daddy roared, "Hey, what a helluva name for the club."

Not too long after he named the club he traded it for a restaurant, losing money at the time, which was owned by Enrico Banducci. Banducci was a wildly generous man who demonstratively loved his friends—his restaurant was failing because he was giving away too much food. He took on the hungry i, which wasn't worth much at that time, and turned it into a roaring success.

In keeping with the idea of the "inner man's search," Enrico thought that there should be "no big frills at the club" so the visitor could feel that "right now you're what counts. Not how it looks, or any diamonds you're wearing. But [it's] the inner man that counts." If you had been here while Banducci was in charge, you would have found only a plain room with an exposed brick wall and director's chairs around small tables.

A Who's Who of nightclub entertainers began their careers at the original hungry i, including Lenny Bruce, Billie Holiday (who first sang "Strange Fruit" here), Bill Cosby, Richard Pryor, Woody Allen, and Barbra Streisand.

Head back to Columbus Avenue and turn left. Look for the:

8. **Purple Onion,** at 140 Columbus Avenue. Many famous headliners have played here (often before they were famous), including Phyllis Diller (now so big that she's famous for something as simple as her laugh), who was still struggling when she played a two-week engagement in the late '50s. Alex Haley tried to interview her during that engagement, and she told him, "No, not yet baby. I'm not big enough for you to be able to sell it, and you're not big enough to get it sold in the right place." Six years later, while working as a reporter for the *Saturday Evening Post,* Haley saw that Diller

was playing at the hungry i, so he went in and knocked on her dressing room door. She jumped out of her chair and hugged him, saying, "Baby, we've made it." She was also one of the first people to contact Haley after his success with *Roots*.

Maya Angelou, author of *I Know Why the Caged Bird Sings* and the poet who read at the inauguration of President Clinton, also sang here in the 1950s.

Continue up Columbus Avenue for a look at:

9. **Columbus Tower.** You'll see it on your left at the intersection of Pacific Avenue, but if you walk a little farther then turn around and look back down Columbus, you'll be able to get a better look at this flat-iron building erected between 1905 and 1907, which was bought and restored by movie director and producer Francis Ford Coppola in the 1970s.

Go right on Pacific Avenue, and just after you cross Montgomery Street you'll be at Osgood Place (an alley), on the left, which is now registered as a Historic Landmark and as a result is one of the few quiet little alleyways left in the city. Go through Osgood and go left on Broadway to:

10. **1010 Montgomery Street** (at the corner of Montgomery and Broadway). *Note:* Don't waste your energy climbing the hill that extends up Montgomery from here—you'll need it later for Telegraph Hill. This is where Allen Ginsberg lived during the time he wrote his legendary poem *Howl.*

Ginsberg first performed *Howl* on October 13, 1955, in this converted auto-repair shop at the corner of Fillmore and Union streets (see Walking Tour 8, stop 15 for the exact location). Called the Six Gallery, the auto-repair shop was fitted with a small stage and chairs in a half-circle for a reading by six poets. The rest of the garage was set up to hold approximately 100 people.

Scheduled to read that night were Kenneth Rexroth, Philip Lamantia, Michael McClure, Philip Whalen, Allen Ginsberg, and Gary Snyder, in that order. Up until Ginsberg got up to read, the event had been rather innocuous as far as those things went; Jack Kerouac had brought enough California burgundy to keep everyone happy, and people were relaxed and enjoying themselves.

A little drunk and a little nervous, Ginsberg began the first public reading of *Howl*. He quickly fell into the rhythm of the poem, swaying to one side as he began each line and back and forth with each word until he emerged breathless at the end of the line only to be pushed onward to the next with a deep breath and an enthusiastic Jack Kerouac's explosive "Go!"

By the time he finished reading he was crying and the audience was going wild. Rexroth cried along with Ginsberg, and Jack Kerouac said, "Ginsberg, this poem will make you famous in San Francisco." Rexroth was more visionary when he said it would make him famous not only in San Francisco, but "from bridge to bridge." Michael McClure has described *Howl* as "Allen's metamorphosis from a quiet brilliant burning bohemian scholar, trapped by his flames and repressions, to epic bard."

The reading at the Six Gallery did more than make Ginsberg famous, it also made the rest of the major players famous, and catapulted the Beat poets into the limelight.

Continue along Broadway toward Columbus Avenue. This particular stretch of Broadway is San Francisco's answer to New York's Times Square, complete with strip clubs and peep shows, and it has always had a reputation as a red light district. In fact, before World War I this area was known as the "Barbary Coast" and was filled with brothels and sleazy fleabag hotels. In the 1950s the area was cleaned up and Broadway made more accessible to traffic and therefore more conducive to nightclubs of a slightly less noxious genre.

Along the way, on the right side of the street, you'll come to Columbus Books, which sells new and used discount books and is worth a quick trip inside.

Keep going on Broadway, and along the way you'll pass the current location of the hungry i. When you get to the corner of Broadway and Columbus Avenue you will also see the:

11. **Condor Club,** where Carol Doda scandalously bared her breasts and danced topless for the first time in 1964 (note the bronze plaque). Go inside and have a look at the framed newspaper clippings that hang around the dining room.

From the back room you can see Doda's old dressing-room door and a reproduction of the piano that would descend from the second floor with her atop it.

The Condor Club credits itself with having started the strip joint craze that took off after completely nude dancers were seen here. The section of Broadway that was home to these "joints" became known as "The Strip."

When you leave the Condor Club, cross to the south side of Broadway. Note the mural of jazz musicians directly across Columbus. Across Columbus Avenue, diagonally across the intersection from the Condor Club, is:

12. **City Lights Bookstore,** at 261 Columbus Avenue. Owned by another Beat poet, Lawrence Ferlinghetti, City Lights was the first all-paperback bookstore in San Francisco and is now a city landmark—one of the last of the Beat-era hangouts in operation. The building dates from 1907, but the Beats (and Ferlinghetti) didn't move in until 1953. At that time, most people thought that paperback books were inferior to hardcovers in both the quality of the paper and the quality of the content, but Ferlinghetti forced people to think differently about them. He made great literature available to everyone by stocking his bookstore with less costly editions.

As an active member in the Beat movement, Ferlinghetti established his shop as a meeting place where writers could attend poetry readings and other events. It's still a vibrant part of the literary scene in San Francisco, and an entire room is devoted to the Beats.

Ferlinghetti has always been a maverick bookseller (and also a publisher). He was the first to publish and sell Allen Ginsberg's controversial poem *Howl,* and his arrest in 1957 for selling obscene materials brought the bookstore to the attention of the general public. Ferlinghetti was acquitted when the judge ruled that *Howl* had "redeeming social value." To this day there is still a City Lights Press, and Ferlinghetti continues to publish new and controversial writers.

Down from City Lights Bookstore, across aptly named Jack Kerouac Street (on the same side of Columbus Avenue) is:

13. **Vesuvio Café.** Because of its proximity to City Lights Bookstore, Vesuvio became a favorite hangout of the Beats. Originally opened in 1949 by Frenchman Henri Lenoir, Vesuvio once advertised the sale of the Beatnik Kit, and in the front window was displayed a mannequin wearing a black sweater, sunglasses, a mustache, and a pair of sandals. Dylan Thomas used to drink here; so did Jack Kerouac, Ferlinghetti, Ginsberg, and all the others. Even today, Vesuvio Café still maintains its original bohemian atmosphere.

   You'll probably still see a couple of regulars hanging out in the front window playing cards or reading the newspaper, and the walls are hung with the art of local artists just as they were when Lenoir was still in charge. There's a sign over the bar explaining that no food is served on the premises, but any visitors are welcome to bring their lunch and have a drink. Also over the bar is a ribald quotation: "T'was a woman that drove me to drink and I never had the decency to thank her." You can even order drinks named after the Beats, like the "Jack Kerouac."

   Facing Vesuvio's across Columbus Avenue are two other favorite spots of the Beat Generation:

14. **Spec's Adler Museum Café** and **Tosca Café** (if you're facing both Spec's and Tosca from City Lights Bookstore, Tosca's is to the right down Columbus). Spec's (down William Saroyan Place) was also owned by Henri Lenoir, and today it's a lively spot frequented by a new generation of artists and writers. Go inside this small wooden bar and you'll find a friendly crowd, as well as a "museum" that consists of a few glass cases filled with memorabilia brought back and dropped off by various seamen who have frequented the pub with its ceiling-hung maritime flags and exposed brick walls.

   Tosca's down-to-earth atmosphere has, for many years, attracted the city's most creative types.

   From here, go up Columbus across Broadway to Grant Avenue, where you should turn right, walking until you come to Vallejo Street. At 606 Vallejo Street (at the corner of Vallejo Street and Grant Avenue) is:

15. **Caffe Trieste,** yet another favorite spot of the Beats. Opened in 1954, it is probably the oldest coffeehouse on the West Coast, and still a local favorite. If you're here on Saturday you might be lucky enough to catch a live opera performance by the owner's family.

    Go left out of Caffe Trieste onto Vallejo Street, continuing toward Stockton Street. On your way you'll pass a wonderful shop called:

16. **Biordi Art Imports,** on your right at 412 Columbus Avenue. Since you're in the heart of San Francisco's Italian neighborhood, you might want to stop in here to admire (or purchase) the majolica and hand-painted Italian dinnerware. Open since 1946, Biordi hand-picks its artisans, and in their catalog you'll find biographies of those who are currently represented.

    When you get to Stockton Street go right and look for the Eureka Bank at 1435 Stockton Street (between Vallejo and Green). On the second floor of the bank you'll find the:

17. **North Beach Museum,** displaying historical artifacts that tell the story of North Beach, Chinatown, and Fisherman's Wharf. Just before you enter the museum you'll find a framed, handwritten poem by Lawrence Ferlinghetti that captures his impressions of this primarily Italian neighborhood. After you pass through the glass doors you'll find many photographs of some of the first Chinese and Italian immigrants, as well as pictures of San Francisco after the 1906 earthquake. You can visit the museum any time the bank is open, and admission is free.

    Before continuing, stop at the corner of Green Street, Stockton Street, and Columbus Avenue, and look down Columbus to the right (as you exit from the front of the bank); there you'll see the:

18. **R. Matteuchi Street Clock.** An interesting landmark, this clock was originally located outside a jewelry store of the same name. This is just one of several street clocks that can be found in San Francisco, and it's a wonderful, elegant reminder of the past. If you'd like a closer look, which you

probably will, go ahead—just know that you'll have to come back here when you're done.

If you went to see the clock, backtrack up Columbus Avenue and go left on Green Street to:

19. **Fugazi Hall,** at 678 Green Street (between Columbus and Powell Streets). It doesn't look like much from the outside, but Fugazi Hall was donated to the city (and more importantly, the North Beach area) by John Fugazi, the founder of the Italian bank that was taken over by A. P. Giannini and turned into the original Transamerica Corporation.

For many years, Fugazi Hall has been staging the zany and whimsical musical revue *Beach Blanket Babylon.* The show evolved from Steve Silver's Rent-a-Freak service, which consisted of a group of party-goers who would attend parties dressed as any number of characters in extraordinary costumes. The fun caught on, and soon came *Beach Blanket Babylon.*

If you love comedy, you'll love this show. I don't want to spoil it for you by telling you what it's about, but if you get tickets (and it is sometimes possible to get tickets even at the last minute on weekdays), you should arrive fairly early because you'll be seated around small cocktail tables on a first-come, first-serve basis. You'll want to be as close to the stage as possible. This show is definitely worth the price of admission.

Continue along Green Street to Powell Street and go right on Powell to Union Street. Go right again.

Take a Break **Little City Antipasti,** at 673 Union Street, is a great place to take a refreshment stop. It's informal and the food is excellent. You can make a meal just on the antipasti here. If you're a garlic lover, and I mean *lover,* you must try the roasted bulb of garlic and brie.

As you come out of Little City Antipasti, you'll be right in front of:

20. **Washington Square,** one of the oldest parks in the city. This land was designated a public park in 1847 and has undergone many changes since then. Its current landscaping dates from 1955. Even though it's called a "square," this

little oasis in the middle of such a bustling neighborhood sort of lost its square status when Columbus Avenue was laid out and one of its four corners was lopped off.

You'll notice **Saints Peter and Paul Church,** which is the religious center for this neighborhood's Italian community, to your left. Designed in 1922, the cathedral took 20 years to build. Known as "the Church of the Fishermen" (because it is the primary church for the Italian fishermen who lived here), it is the point of origin for processions that honor the blessing of the fishing fleet every October. Take a few moments to go inside and check out the traditional Italian interior. Also note that this is the church in which baseball great Joe DiMaggio married his first wife. He wasn't allowed to marry Marilyn Monroe here because he had been divorced. He married Monroe at City Hall and went here for publicity photos.

On the Columbus Avenue side of the park you'll find a bronze statue erected in 1933 to honor San Francisco's firemen at the bequest of Lillie Hitchcock Coit (See Walking Tour 4, stop 4 for more information).

A statue of Benjamin Franklin, donated by H. D. Cogswell (a dentist and prohibitionist) in 1879, stands at the center of the park over a time capsule. Emptied in 1979, the capsule previously held a number of Victorian tracts. Currently the capsule is home to a pair of Levi's jeans, a bottle of wine, a Ferlinghetti poem, and a Hoodoo Rhythm Devils album. Chances are that you won't be around for the next opening—it's in 2079.

Across at the other side of the park—on the Stockton Street side—is a bench with a plaque in dedication to Irving Stone, Jack London's biographer, who was born near here in 1903.

Today the park is a pleasant place to sit and watch children play, toss a Frisbee, or chat with a retired Italian octogenarian who has seen the city grow and change. From here you can see the famous Coit Tower at the top of Telegraph Hill to the northwest.

This is the end of the North Beach tour, but you can begin the tour of Telegraph Hill, which begins on the next page, from here. If you're very tired, I would suggest that you wait for at least an hour before you begin the ascent to the top of Telegraph Hill—it's a fairly strenuous walk, and you'll probably only end up cursing me, this book, yourself, and all the tour buses that pass you on their way up if you don't take a break.

TELEGRAPH HILL

Start: Washington Square.

Public Transportation: 15, 30, 41, or 45 bus.

Finish: Levi Strauss Plaza.

Time: 2 to 3 hours, not including shopping time.

Best Times: After 10am, but before 3pm so you'll get a chance to go into Coit Tower.

Worst Times: Before 10am and after 3pm.

Hills That Could Kill: The Kearny Street hill that takes you up to Telegraph Hill Boulevard. There's no avoiding this one.

ising sharply from the streets of neighboring North Beach is Telegraph Hill, named for the semaphore that was installed at its peak in 1850 to alert the city to ships' arrivals. The whole city would stop when the semaphore raised its arms in signal that the Pacific Mail Steamship Company's side-wheel was on its way. Hubert Howe Bancroft, a pioneer bookseller, wrote in his eight-volume history of California that "when the signal flag was unfurled, and the windmill-looking indicator on Telegraph Hill stretched forth its long ungainly wooden arms and told the town of a steamer outside, a thrill went through the heart."

In the 1850s, in addition to the semaphore, the hill was home to many of the city's criminals, but the Vigilance Committee eventually ran them out of town. Later, when the Gold Rush was in full swing, Chilean and Peruvian groups claimed the hill as home, followed later by the Irish, who, when they moved to the Mission District, were supplanted by the Italians.

The fire of 1906 came swiftly to Telegraph Hill, and legend has it that the efforts of some of the Italian residents to douse the flames with 500 barrels of red wine saved many of the homes on the hill. Because they were able to save their homes, most people living on Telegraph Hill thought they were safe—that is, until four months later when the Gray brothers began dynamiting their property to quarry rock out of the hill. The blasts shook the entire hill and even lopped off portions of various hill dwellers' lots. Residents were furious and some tried to take legal action to stop the Gray brothers from ruining their property. The court system didn't help and the battle raged on. Finally, George Gray was killed by one of his former employees, and that was the end of quarrying on the hill.

Well before the shooting of George Gray, the residents were interested in preserving Telegraph Hill, but it wasn't until the 1920s that the Park Commission made an effort in that direction. The road leading to the top of the hill was paved, and an incredibly ugly balustrade punctuated with giant urns (that only served to block the beautiful view) was erected alongside the road. Once again, residents came together in a fury, and the Park Commission was forced to remove the balustrade.

Between the time the Park Commission took the balustrade down and 1933, when Coit Tower was erected, Telegraph Hill became a haven for artists. They were attracted to the hill because it was an inexpensive and beautiful place to live, and they loved it in spite of (and probably because of) the fact that they had to live in wooden shacks and studio apartments. Some people referred to Telegraph Hill during this time as the "Montparnasse of the West."

Like most other artists' communities, this one was discovered by a group of "wanna-be's" and Telegraph Hill became the trendy place to live in the mid-1930s. The artists, who couldn't afford the new, higher rents, were driven out.

Today, Telegraph Hill has its share of ugly apartment buildings, but it has been able to retain some of its charm, and as you walk this tour you'll go by some of the oldest houses on the hill, climbing wooden steps and walking the wooden boardwalks of Napier Lane. You'll also go into Coit Tower, where you can admire the view and the murals within. Finally, you'll end up at Levi Strauss Plaza where the jeans company is headquartered.

This is a rough walk, so proceed only when you're feeling well-rested.

• • • • • • • • • • • • • • • •

Exit Washington Square via the intersection of Union and Stockton streets. Go left on Union Street (with the square at your back) to Grant Avenue. Go right on Grant and begin this tour with a little shopping.

1. **Grant Avenue shopping.** This section of Grant holds a variety of shopping experiences. Begin by stopping in at the Primal Art Center at 1422 Grant Avenue, on your left. Here you'll find all kinds of sculptures and artifacts from Africa and Papua New Guinea, including masks and jewelry.

Just a bit farther along, on the same side of the street, is the Schlock Shop (1418 Grant Avenue), which is simply crammed full of just about anything you can imagine. As you squeeze into the small, dark shop you might go on sensory overload, so be careful. You could spend hours picking your way through all the "schlock" in here.

Continuing along Grant Avenue, cross Green Street to No. 1353 on the right, the Lost & Found Saloon. Even though it looks like a dump, the Lost & Found Saloon was once another favorite spot of the Beats and was called the Coffee Gallery. Today, it hosts some great live jazz and blues artists on a regular basis.

Figone Hardware at No. 1351 is your last stop on Grant Avenue. Inside you'll find your average everyday hardware store items, like shovels, pliers, pipes, and paint, but you'll also find some kitchen items that were designed specifically for Italian cooking, like ravioli makers and cannoli stuffers.

When you've finished browsing at Figone, turn around and head back to Green Street. Go right to:

2. **377 Green Street,** the former home of Kenneth Patchen (1911–1972) and his wife, Miriam. Patchen was born in Ohio and educated in Arkansas. He started out as a poet, incorporating jazz rhythms and phrasing into his verse. He is credited with being the first poet to experiment along those lines.

   He was also a painter, and he often designed the covers for his books of poetry. His drawings and paintings have a whimsical, childlike quality about it. Patchen was awarded a Guggenheim fellowship in 1936.

   Backtrack to Kearny Street and turn right. After you cross Union Street, you will come to:

3. **1425 Kearny Street,** where Richard Brautigan (1935–1984), a California author who wrote *Trout Fishing in America* (1967) and *In Watermelon Sugar* (1968), is said to have lived at the end of the 1960s. The story has it that while he was in residence he decorated the toilet seat with paintings of trout.

   After you pass the former Brautigan house, continue up this monster of a hill to the steps that will take you to Telegraph Hill Boulevard. At the top of the stairs after you catch your breath, go right along Telegraph Hill Boulevard, following it until you get to:

4. **Coit Tower,** the white, fluted pillar that was constructed after the death of Lillie Hitchcock Coit with money she had left to the city of San Francisco. She stated in her will that the money was "to be expended in an appropriate manner for the purpose of adding to the beauty of the city which I have always loved." She didn't leave any other specific instructions.

   In 1931, after the balustrade fiasco, it was decided that Lillie Coit's money would be used to construct a memorial tower on Telegraph Hill, and the view from the top of the tower was not to be obscured by any other building. This would ensure the preservation of Telegraph Hill that residents had been seeking. Since they only had $125,000 to devote to the construction of the memorial, they had to use inexpensive building materials. The cheapest at that time was reinforced concrete.

Telegraph Hill

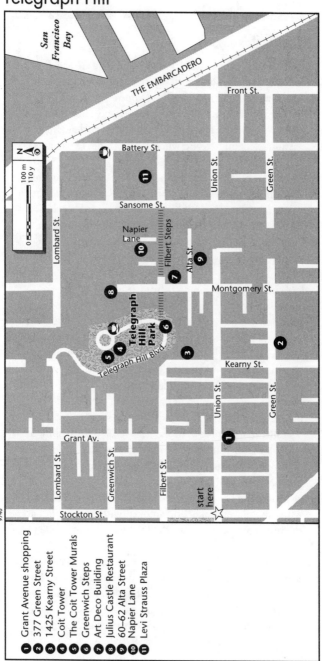

① Grant Avenue shopping
② 377 Green Street
③ 1425 Kearny Street
④ Coit Tower
⑤ The Coit Tower Murals
⑥ Greenwich Steps
⑦ Art Deco Building
⑧ Julius Castle Restaurant
⑨ 60–62 Alta Street
⑩ Napier Lane
⑪ Levi Strauss Plaza

Lillie Coit

Lillie Hitchcock Coit (1844–1929) came to San Francisco from Maryland at the age of seven. Soon after arriving in the city, she was a victim of one of the first fires San Francisco ever saw. Lillie was able to escape, but her friends were not. The fire and the deaths of her friends had a lasting effect on her, and when she was older (a teenager), Coit happened to pass the Knickerbocker Engine Company No. 5 of the Volunteer Fire Department, on their way up Telegraph Hill to douse a fire. Realizing that they could use an extra pair of hands, Lillie dropped her schoolbooks and called all the men within earshot to help her as she began pulling the tow rope. Because of her help Engine No. 5 was the first to get to the top of Telegraph Hill.

The Volunteer Firemen from Engine No. 5 were so impressed with her that they made her their mascot. From that day onward she would race with them to fires, and in parades she always rode on top of the Knickerbocker engine. In 1863 they made her an honorary member and gave her a diamond-studded badge with "No. 5" written on it. After that she embroidered the number 5 on all her clothing and she signed her name Lillie Hitchcock 5 and always attended the annual firemen's banquet.

Lillie married Howard Coit in 1868, and in spite of the fact that he came from a rich Connecticut family, she continued to attend functions with the firemen of Engine No. 5. You might wonder how she behaved at elegant social functions—the answer is same way she did when she played poker and smoked with her buddies at the fire department, of course. (She was also an excellent shot.)

When her husband died in 1885, she moved away from San Francisco for a time. After she finally returned to San Francisco she was the unfortunate witness to a murder and couldn't bear to live here anymore, so she moved to Paris. San Francisco drew her back in 1924 at age 83, and she died in a sanatorium here in 1929. She was cremated with her diamond-studded "No. 5" badge.

Many criticized the plan for the tower, saying that it was ugly. Even Gertrude Atherton, author and friend of Lillie Hitchcock Coit, argued against the memorial, stating that Coit particularly despised towers. A petition against the building of the tower was signed by 464 people. Nonetheless, it was built, and it stands today at 212 feet.

In spite of the fact that the tower seems to resemble the nozzle of a fire hose, the architects, Henry Howard and Arthur Brown, Jr., claim that the resemblance was never intended.

Head into the tower, but before you ascend to the top, let's take a look at the murals on the ground floor; they were painted between 1933 and 1934 as part of the Public Works of Art Project (PWAP), a pilot program for the WPA.

5. **The Coit Tower murals.** Soon after Lillie Hitchcock Coit died the Depression hit, and with the New Deal came government-sponsored projects to help artists and writers survive. A program similar to those of the Works Projects Administration (WPA), which was to emerge a year later, the PWAP commissioned artists to paint, among other things, frescoes (or murals) on the walls of public or government buildings. After Coit Tower was built, it was designated a recipient of this artwork.

Though they numbered close to 30, the artists who worked on Coit Tower were a fairly unified group. Several of them had been students of Mexican muralist Diego Rivera, who was also a political radical with strong ties to Russian Communists. It is in his favored form—the traditional Mexican-style fresco—that the murals were painted; and it is likely that several of the artists sympathized with his politics, too. But the very medium they chose to work in also required that they collaborate on both the scale of their work and their palette.

The consistent scale was important because if some artists worked on large figures while others worked on miniatures, the individual murals would not have formed a cohesive unit, essential in a building like Coit Tower which has no separate rooms. And because the technique of fresco required the hand-mixing of a range of earth tones, the palette had to be agreed upon before work began. Only one artists' assistant was given the privilege of grinding and mixing the pigments, simply to assure the uniformity of color.

The technique of fresco is complex. It begins with a mixture of fine marble dust and slaked lime, with which the wall is coated and re-coated until an acceptable surface has been prepared. When the surface is dry and hard, the artist comes in and paints a dark (maybe even black) outline of the figures and shapes to be painted. On the following morning, a section of the wall is covered in a thin layer of wet plaster. The artist then comes in and begins to paint, with a small brush, on the wet plaster. When the plaster dries, the paint dries, and the painting actually becomes part of the wall. If a mistake is made in painting and it has dried before the artist realizes the mistake, the paint and plaster must actually be chiseled or chipped off the wall and the whole process must be repeated. Because the plaster dilutes the intensity of the color, several layers have to be applied before a uniform intensity is achieved.

As you enter the tower, you will see directly ahead of you the first mural, *Animal Force and Machine Force* by Ray Boynton. It measures 10 feet by 36 feet and displays both rural (on the left of the door) and urban (to the right of the door) scenes of California. In 1917, Boynton, a professor of Art at the University of California at Berkeley, became one of the first to work with the fresco medium in San Francisco. This mural includes one of the most interesting, almost mystical features of all the murals in the tower—the eyes of "Old Man Weather" above the doorway.

Go to the right and turn around so that you're looking at the wall by the door through which you entered. This mural, *California Industrial Scenes,* was created by John Langley Howard, who was once a member of the Art Students' League in New York. This is his only known fresco.

As you continue around you'll find William Hesthal's *Railroad and Shipping* fresco, which attempts to show the effects of the New Deal on the depressed economy of the 1930s. Hesthal was a student of the California School of Fine Arts, and some of his works are housed at the San Francisco Museum of Fine Arts.

The Surveyor and *The Steelworker,* by Clifford Wight, are located one on each side of the windows on the wall to your right. Unfortunately, it is now impossible to see the impact that Wight originally had on Coit Tower, because his Communist slogan (which caused the Tower to be closed during the summer of 1934) has since been erased. The controversy came about over a piece of cable bent to look like a sickle, a hammer, and the slogan, "United Workers of the World," the universal symbol of Communism.

On the left you'll see Ralph Stackpole's *Industries of California*. Stackpole was the teacher of Frederick Law Olmsted and a student of the Ecole des Beaux-Arts in Paris. Stackpole once said that he would like to see San Francisco dubbed "The City of Frescoes." With all the murals around town today I wouldn't be surprised if the city has earned that title.

The next mural, *Newsgathering,* was done by Suzanne Scheuer. There are some intricately painted elements involved in this fresco, among them the painting of the newspaper on the window ledge and the depiction of the color process of making a comic strip (around the window). The painting shows the making of a newspaper from editorial to the printing and selling of the latest edition. You'll probably notice that this painting is a bit brighter than the first few you saw; that's because Scheuer had a greater preference for reds and blues than the other artists.

In the same corner, on the other wall, is a painting of the inside of the public library by Bernard B. Zakheim, a Polish immigrant who came to San Francisco seeking political asylum. He studied at the Mark Hopkins Art Institute (now the San Francisco Art Institute) and painted his first fresco at the Jewish Community Center. He was instrumental in organizing the Coit Tower project.

The next two panels on either side of the windows, by Mallette Dean, depict a stockbroker (some think it's A. P. Giannini, see Tour 2, stop 5 for details) and a scientist. Dean studied at the California School of Fine Arts and worked for many years as a label designer in the California wine industry. Some of his work is housed at the San Francisco Museum of Art.

Turn around to the wall facing the windows and you'll find yourself transported into a street scene entitled *City Life* by Victor Arnautoff. A Russian, Arnautoff spent 30 years in the United States and studied under Diego Rivera. The intersection shown here is that of Montgomery and Washington streets.

George Harris is responsible for the painting of the next panel to your right as you continue to walk around, and it's titled *Banking and the Law.* Some of the titles on the books in the law library are very amusing. Harris attended the California School of Fine Arts and was one of the youngest to work on the Coit Tower project.

The adjacent panel is called *Department Store,* and it was executed by Frede Vidar. Born in Denmark but transplanted to San Francisco in 1923 at the age of 12, he studied at the California School of Fine Arts and once had the good fortune of studying with Matisse while in Paris in 1933. The department store scene depicted here is typical of the 1930s, with soda fountain and all.

As you approach the next group of windows you'll be passing into the agriculture section of the tower and you'll be greeted by Clifford Wight's *Farmer and Cowboy.* Wight, who also painted *The Surveyor* and *The Steelworker,* is thought to have been a student of Diego Rivera.

Another woman artist, Maxine Albro, painted *California,* the fresco opposite the windows. Also a student of Diego Rivera, she studied at the California School of Fine Arts before leaving for Mexico to study with Rivera. Unfortunately a lot of her work has been destroyed, but happily, this apricot-, orange-, and flower-picking agricultural scene survives.

In the final corner you'll find Ray Bertrand's *Meat Industry* mural, whose gray tones and flesh colors are in direct contrast with the vibrant, brightly colored outdoor scene that you just saw. Bertrand, a native San Franciscan, was also a student at the California School of Fine Arts, and most of his work was lithography and landscape painting.

The final mural of note here is adjacent to Bertrand's mural and is titled *California Agricultural Industry.* The artist, Gordon Langdon, joined his mural with Bertrand's through subject matter because of their proximity. On one side you see the meat-packing industry, and here you see the actual farm where the animals are raised. Note the man in the silo peeking out the window.

Now that you've finished your tour around the tower, head up to the top for the view from the observation deck.

When you're finished upstairs, head down from the observation deck and back out to the parking area and circle out front.

☕ Take a Break Because they know people are exhausted by the time they get to the top of Telegraph Hill, and because there's always a huge number of tourists up here and nowhere to eat, street food vendors are often parked out in front of the tower. Don't expect anything much more than a soda or an ice cream, though.

Begin going back down the way you came up. Before long, around to your left you will find the:

6. **Greenwich Steps,** a perfectly pleasant way to descend the hill. These flights of steps make up one of San Francisco's most charming spots, and in spite of the fact that you have to go a little bit out of your way to find them, it's worth it.

Wend your way down the wooden steps and through the flowers and shrubs. After you've passed several Victorian cottages, you'll come to a sort of landing, which is actually the upper level of Montgomery Street.

Go right for a few steps and cross to the other side of Montgomery Street. From here you'll get the best view of the:

7. **Art Deco Building,** at 1360 Montgomery Street. Built in 1936, this four-story building was one of the filming locations for Bogie and Bacall's *Dark Passage*.

Go back in the other direction past the steps you just came down, and when you get to the hairpin turn in the road that leads you down to the lower level of Montgomery Street you'll be standing in front of the:

8. **Julius Castle Restaurant,** at 1541 Montgomery Street. Built in 1921, this cliff-hanging establishment is better appreciated for its view than its food. The restaurant used to have a turntable for cars out front because it was too difficult to turn a car around at this particular point on Montgomery Street. This is a particularly enjoyable spot for a romantic dinner.

Continue around, and as you approach the corner of the Filbert Steps, keep going (however, you should know that you will be returning to this spot) and head on to Alta Street. Go left to:

9. **60–62 Alta Street,** the former home of gay author Armistead Maupin. Originally from Raleigh, North Carolina, Maupin began his career as an author through a serial story in the *San Francisco Chronicle* in 1976. The series of articles was called "Tales of the City" and was widely followed by San Franciscans and out-of-towners who obtained their copies of the story from their San Franciscan friends. Many readers thought they saw themselves in the stories since it was widely known that Maupin based the tales in part on his own experiences in San Francisco's social scene.

From Anna Madrigal, the pot-smoking/growing landlady of 28 Barbary Lane (a fictional lane in San Francisco) to Mary Ann Singleton, a particularly naive midwesterner who heads for San Francisco to get away from her small-town friends and family; to Michael Tolliver (or Mouse) a gay man in search of true love, Maupin takes us through his characters' lives (and in turn our own) as he weaves his splendidly comical tales.

Maupin gathered all his 1976 stories together and the revised and edited tales were issued as one volume, *Tales of the City.* He followed that volume with another, *More Tales of the City,* and another, *Further Tales of the City.* After that the titles changed a little bit, but many of the same characters remained. The final three struck a more serious chord with the onset of AIDS. They were *Babycakes, Sure of You,* and finally, *Significant Others.* The first book has been adapted for television as a PBS series.

Once you begin reading these books you won't be able to put them down. You'll promise yourself that you're only going to read one more chapter. You'll read that one and another and another, until you suddenly realize it's four in the morning and you've finished the entire book.

If you follow Alta Street to the end you'll find yourself precariously perched at the edge of a precipice, so if you're afraid of heights, don't go. However, you'll be treated to a spectacular vista if you do.

When you're finished admiring the view, go back out to Montgomery Street and go right back to the second half of the Filbert Steps. Go right down the wooden steps. The second alley on your left is:

10. **Napier Lane,** which is probably one of the only short boardwalk alleys left in the entire city of San Francisco. It is thought that at one time sailors were shanghaied here. On the corner of Napier Lane at 222 Filbert Street there once was a grocery store and a saloon. You're sure to see many cats wandering the boardwalk, and quite a few more as you continue to descend the Filbert Steps.

Continue down the Filbert Steps. As you head down the last set of steps, which turn to concrete, you'll see, to your right, a cliffside area that looks as though it's under construction. A former rock quarry, this area proved to be quite profitable for excavation, but unfortunately, a couple of houses fell off the cliff into the pit and excavation had to be stopped.

When you get to the bottom of the stairs, go straight, crossing Sansome Street into:

11. **Levi Strauss Plaza,** where you'll find the headquarters for Levi Strauss & Co. If you go inside the building on your right you can see exhibits that include designs of old Levi's jeans, including some examples of the first pairs ever made.

Ever noticed the initials S.F. on the rivets of Levi's jeans? They stand for San Francisco. Another interesting note about the rivets on Levi's jeans is that they were originally put there in an effort to extend the life of the pants. The first work pants designed by Levi's were made for miners whose heavy pockets (loaded with the fruits of their labors) ripped all too often. The rivets strengthened the pockets and were not intended as decorative features.

You'll also get to see one of Levi's failed projects—brightly colored women's jeans that were advertised along with lemon, lime, and orange Jell-O gelatin products. For obvious reasons they weren't well received by the public.

Winding Down After you exit the corporate head-quarters, cross the street on the other side of the plaza, where you'll find, at 1300 Battery Street, one of San Francisco's most famous restaurants—the **Fog City Diner.** If you'd like to sample the fare, you should probably make a reservation in advance. You might be able to get in for lunch, but don't be surprised if you can't.

NOB HILL

Start: Corner of Jones and California streets.

Public Transportation: You can take the California Line Cable Car to the corner of Jones and California streets, or you can take the No. 1 bus to Jones and Sacramento streets and walk one block over to California Street.

Finish: Corner of Taylor and Clay streets.

Time: 2 hours.

Best Times: Between 10am and 5pm.

Worst Times: Before 10am or after 5pm.

Hills That Could Kill: Do not climb up Jones or Taylor streets between Bush and California streets unless you're physically fit. The block of Taylor between Pine and California streets has a 23.7 percent grade. If you're looking for a particularly good workout, go on up (and if you need to rest, you can just lean against the hill).

Rising 338 feet above sea level and bounded roughly by Pine, Pacific, Stockton, and Polk streets, Nob Hill is one of the highest and most well-known of San Francisco's many hills.

In the beginning it was only well-known because of its height, and it was occupied by the poor because the rich didn't want to climb the treacherously sandy hill to reach their homes. So, instead of the mansions you see today, a series of wooden shacks dotted the hill in the early 1800s.

Beginning in the 1850s a few more prosperous merchants and doctors sought refuge from the turmoil of life on Montgomery Street. In fact, the first person to move to the hill was a doctor by the name of Hayne. He was followed by Senator George Hearst (father of William Randolph), and a merchant by the name of William Walton.

Hallidie's invention of the cable car in the 1870s (San Francisco's Golden Era) made the hills much more accessible, and those first forward-looking residents were soon followed by a long line of millionaires who recognized the potential value of the real estate atop the hill. They included, among others, the Big Four (Crocker, Hopkins, Huntington, and Stanford) who built the Central (later Southern) Pacific Railroad, and the Bonanza Kings (O'Brien, Flood, Fair, and Mackay) who struck it rich with the Comstock Lode. They were the "nabobs" who gave Nob Hill its name.

The original Big Four began making their money as shopkeepers who sold supplies to the miners during the Gold Rush. Leland Stanford had been a grocer in Sacramento, Charlie Crocker, a dry-goods clerk, Collis P. Huntington and Mark Hopkins, sellers of hardware. At heart they were simple men who wanted to lead simple lives. Then, with the building of the railroad in 1869, they struck it really rich.

After they decided to move to Nob Hill, the Stanfords set about building a simple but dignified home. Mark Hopkins would have done the same, but his wife, 20 years his junior, worked her charms on him until he gave her carte blanche to design whatever she desired. Crocker also built an ornate mansion that stood on the site of present-day Grace Cathedral. Huntington and Flood (the latter was originally a saloonkeeper who later made his fortune from the Comstock Lode) also built mansions of their own. "Bonanza Jim" Fair, though, never completed his planned mansion on the hill—his marriage ended in divorce before he got the chance.

Shortly after the mansions were completed, the 1906 earthquake and fire destroyed most of them, except the Flood Mansion, parts of which still stand today. Some of the nabobs rebuilt, but others left. Crocker donated his lot to the Episcopal

Church for the building of a cathedral (now Grace Cathedral). Later, in the 1920s, some of the new mansions were converted into hotels, and Grace Cathedral was begun. With the later construction of some high-rise apartment buildings the hill lost some of its reputation as "Snob Hill," and many middle-class people now live on the sloping sides of the hill (the top, with its high-class hotels, is still reserved for the wealthy).

This tour begins at the summit of Nob Hill and slowly descends the side facing Pacific Heights and the Marina. You'll see the famed Grace Cathedral and walk by the Flood Mansion. You'll also visit the Mark Hopkins and Fairmont hotels, ending the tour at the Cable Car Barn and Museum.

If you're feeling particularly energetic you might want to tie this tour onto the Russian Hill tour, so I have supplied walking directions to the starting point of the Russian Hill tour at the end of this one.

● ● ● ● ● ● ● ● ● ● ● ● ● ● ● ●

On the corner of Jones and California streets you'll see the massive:

1. **Grace Cathedral,** which stands on the site of the old Charles Crocker mansion. Charles Crocker was among the first group of millionaires to build on Nob Hill, and like Mark Hopkins's wife, Crocker stuffed his redwood chateau full of treasures from Europe, including such items as Millet's *The Sower.* He had assembled the lot piecemeal, but there was still a corner owned and occupied by an undertaker named Mr. Yung. Yung saw how much Crocker wanted the land, and when Crocker asked him to sell he demanded an exorbitant sum. Instead of giving in to Mr. Yung's demands, an enraged Crocker built a 40-foot-high "spite fence," depriving Yung of sunlight in an attempt to drive his price down. It worked and Crocker acquired the land, but in 1906, Crocker's redwood mansion was destroyed by the fire that swept the hill. Not long after the fire, Crocker donated his land to the Episcopal diocese.

Enter the Cathedral via the South Portal from California Street.

The original Grace Church stood at the intersection of Powell and Jackson streets and was built in 1849 under the direction of Reverend Dr. John L. Ver Mehr, a Belgian who was the first Episcopal priest in San Francisco. Many of the first parishioners were miners, and when the collection plate was passed they often filled it with gold dust. Later, a bigger church was built at the intersection of Stockton and California streets and was occupied by Bishop Kip, the first Bishop of California. In the 1906 earthquake and fire the third church was destroyed as well, and since it was well known before the fire that the new Bishop, Bishop Nichols, wanted to build a cathedral on a hill, the Crocker family donated their land.

Plans were drawn up for a new cathedral in 1907, and the cornerstone was laid and dedicated three years later. However, work on the present structure didn't begin until 1928. Lewis P. Hobart worked three years designing this primarily French Gothic Cathedral on a cross-shaped plan, but he died 10 years before its completion in 1964.

Grace Cathedral is the third largest Episcopal cathedral in the country, and when you look around, you'll want to look for several oustanding features. Its main doors are stunning replicas of Ghiberti's bronze Doors of Paradise in the Bapistry in Florence. Inside, you will find several brilliant stained-glass windows and a series of religious frescoes. One group of stained-glass windows, designed by Loire Studios of Chartres, depicts modern figures like Judge Thurgood Marshall, poet Robert Frost (a San Francisco native), Albert Einstein, and John Dewey as well as many others. The frescoes, referred to as the World Church Murals, are by Polish-American artist John H. De Rosen and were painted in the late 1940s. The organ dates from 1860, and David Lemon created its Hosea wood sculpture. The Singing Tower (to the right of the main entrance) was given its name because of its incredible 44-bell carillon.

The Cathedral is generally open from about 7:30am to 6 or 7pm every day, and you can visit the gift shop during the day.

Come out of the cathedral the way you entered and go left on California Street to the:

2. **Masonic Temple Auditorium and Museum,** at 1111 California Street. It's a plain white, stone building at the corner of California and Taylor streets. The cornerstone,

Nob Hill

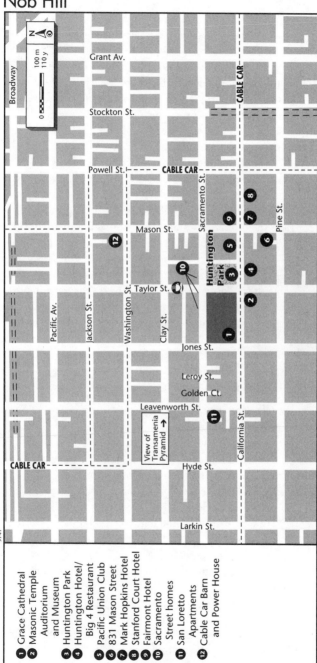

1 Grace Cathedral
2 Masonic Temple
  Auditorium
  and Museum
3 Huntington Park
4 Huntington Hotel/
  Big 4 Restaurant
5 Pacific Union Club
6 831 Mason Street
7 Mark Hopkins Hotel
8 Stanford Court Hotel
9 Fairmont Hotel
10 Sacramento
   Street homes
11 San Loretto
   Apartments
12 Cable Car Barn
   and Power House

which contains a copper casket with historical Masonic and contemporary documents, was dedicated on September 29, 1958.

Before you go inside, note the bas-relief on the left side of the building. The four figures to the left represent each branch of the Armed Forces; the smaller figures represent "a global struggle between the forces of good and evil." The work is dedicated to "Our Masonic Brethren Who Died in the Cause of Freedom."

Enter the building via the short flight of steps between the white marble pillars, and directly ahead of you you'll see the dramatic 45- by 48-foot Endo-Mosaic window, which is made primarily of plastic instead of glass and depicts the history of California Masonry. On the right side of the window are eight vignettes that show scenes from 1840 to the present. In the center are two groupings, the seafarers and wayfarers, representing the two groups that came to California in the 1800s. One of the most important symbols in Freemasonry is the all-seeing eye (which is depicted on our currency); it is featured at the top of the mural.

Upstairs you'll find some historic Masonic articles on display.

Diagonally across the intersection from the temple is:

3. **Huntington Park,** a public oasis in the midst of San Francisco's most prestigious hotels. The park is framed by granite walls that were once a part of the Colton estate.

David Colton, who has never been adequately recognized for his part in the building of the Central (Southern) Pacific Railroad, is perhaps best known for his role in the Great Diamond Hoax of 1871 (see below for details).

The faux-marble Colton mansion was burned in the fire that followed the 1906 earthquake. Huntington, who had purchased the property from Colton in 1892, donated the land to the city after the burned-out lot had stood empty for nine years.

The fountain at the center of the park is said to be a replica of Italy's Tartarughe Fountain in Rome, commissioned by Pope Alexander VII and erected in 1581. Note the *Dancing Sprites* sculpture.

The Great Diamond Hoax of 1871

In 1871 two roughneck miners, Mr. Arnold and Mr. Slack, deposited two bags of what they said were rough-cut diamonds in the Bank of California. Mr. Ralston, the treasurer of the bank, sought them out and persuaded them to sell him a half-share of the mine. Ralston also asked for the right to inspect the property. Arnold and Slack agreed if the inspectors could be blindfolded when they got close to the mine entrance (so that the location of the find would remain a secret). Ralston agreed to be blindfolded and he chose David Colton, who then worked for the Southern Pacific Railroad, as the inspector.

Colton inspected the mine, returning to Ralston trembling with excitement, and poured out several jewels onto the table before his employer. Colton explained that there were so many stones that all he had done was simply bend over and gather them up. The gems were genuine, and a respected mining engineer, Henry Janin, confirmed the value of the mines. Thus, Ralston organized a syndicate, establishing the North American Diamond Company. David Colton was appointed its General Manager, resigning his executive position at the Southern Pacific Railroad.

News of the diamond find traveled, kindling excitement and curiosity. Scientist and scholar Clarence King was so curious that he set out to visit the mines and found ant hills powdered with emerald dust that contained emeralds within, and diamonds in the forks of tree branches. Finally he discovered a partially cut diamond—the mine had been salted! He wired Ralston the news that the mines were a fraud.

Slack disappeared and Arnold returned to Kentucky with the $300,000 that had been paid to him by Ralston and other shareholders, later becoming a banker. Ralston paid back the investors in the diamond business and absorbed a $300,000 personal loss. He later stretched himself so thin financially that he lost all his money. In 1875 he was found bobbing around in San Francisco Bay and is believed to have committed suicide.

Across California Street from Huntington Park is the:

4. Huntington Hotel and **Big 4 Restaurant,** named for railroad magnate Collis P. Huntington. The hotel is one of San Francisco's finest, and inside you'll find no two rooms alike. So elegant is this establishment that if you're a guest in residence here you can ride in style to Union Square or any other shopping district in the hotel's Rolls-Royce.

The Big 4 Restaurant is named for Huntington and his three partners, Hopkins, Stanford, and Crocker, and is decorated with period furnishings that date back to San Francisco's Golden Era.

When you exit the hotel, turn right, continuing down Sacramento Street. Just past Huntington Park on your left is the:

5. Pacific Union Club. Built in 1886 of Connecticut brownstone, this was the original James Flood mansion. Because it was built of stone and not wood, it was one of the few mansions atop Nob Hill to survive the fire of 1906. It was remodeled from 1908–12 by Willis Polk, who added the upper floor and the wings, but the main structure you see today is the original. The bronze fence that surrounds the house is one of the city's most beautiful, and it is told that Flood employed one man just to polish the fence. The original cost of the fence was $30,000.

The Pacific Union Club is a private club—the public is not admitted.

Note that across the street at 1001 California Street (right across the street from the Flood mansion), is the mansion in which Patty Hearst's parents lived during the time that Patty was kidnapped.

Continue along California Street and when you reach Mason Street, turn right. Stay to the left side of Mason as you're facing down the hill. Go about halfway down the block to:

6. 831 Mason Street. This is where the novelist Erskine Caldwell (1903–87) lived some time around 1961. Caldwell was born in Georgia, and his novels, including *Tobacco Road* and *God's Little Acre,* were generally set in the rural south. He was married to Margaret Bourke-White one of the original photographers at *Life* and *Time* magazines.

The Bonanza Kings: O'Brien, Flood, Fair & Mackay

Mining magnate Thomas Henry O'Brien has been described as a simple, kind, unassuming Irishman from Dublin. He was generous and good-natured, widely known as "the Jolly Millionaire." In the summer of 1849 he arrived penniless in San Francisco at the age of 23 and got a job unloading ships in the Bay. The job served him well until the Gold Rush traffic subsided, when he became a clerk in a tobacco and newspaper shop owned by William Hoff. Eventually, he became Hoff's partner.

O'Brien then became friends with store clerk James Clair Flood, a New York–born Irishman, and in 1857 they opened a saloon, the Auction Lunch, at the corner of Pacific and Stockton streets. Later they moved the saloon to 509 Washington Street, just west of Sansome Street, where they offered "free lunch to go with your nickel beer or shot of whiskey." Although the two were very different in temperament—O'Brien loved people and talk while Flood was more withdrawn and businesslike—they forged a good working relationship.

When the San Francisco Mining Exchange moved in a few doors down from the saloon in 1862, their clientele became a source of information. O'Brien and Flood worked the room every evening, picking up tips, eventually amassing quite a fortune. They sold the saloon and became brokers of mining stocks.

They were joined in this venture by John Mackay and James Fair, both mining experts. Mackay was shrewd, but Fair was a driving force in the partnership—hard, vindictive, and determined to make it to the top no matter the price. The four together were unstoppable, and within four years, the business was bringing in about $500,000 a month.

Return to the corner of Mason and California Streets to the:

7. **Mark Hopkins Hotel,** at 999 California Street. One of San Francisco's most opulent mansions once stood here.

After Mark Hopkins struck it rich on the railroad, his wife proceeded to build a mansion with towers, turrets, verandas, porticos, and a Gothic glass conservatory. The result was a hodgepodge of styles: a French chateau with Gothic, Greek, and Arabic details. Nor was the mansion's interior any less ornate. Mrs. Hopkins created an ostentatious display of wealth, exemplified by the decor of the master bedroom, which had ebony walls inlaid with precious stones and ivory.

Mark Hopkins died in 1878, and 15 years later his wife gave their home to the San Francisco Art Institute. Soon after his death, Hopkins's wife married Edward T. Searles, 22 years her junior. When she died, she left the estate to her husband. Mrs. Hopkins's foster son Timothy, who had opposed the marriage, contested the will but settled for $3 million to $4 million. He died in 1891.

Like many other mansions on Nob Hill, this one burned in the fire of 1906; at that time, it was being used by the students of the San Francisco Art Institute, and there are many accounts written of how the students fled with their work under their arms, propping their canvases against other houses that were not yet burning while they rushed in for more.

After the fire the Art Institute sold the land and moved to its current location on Russian Hill (more about the San Francisco Art Institute in Walking Tour 6, stop 13). Not long afterwards the Gothic Revival Mark Hopkins Hotel was erected. It is now famous for, among other things, its rooftop lounge Top of the Mark (a beautiful spot for a drink in the evenings). Gertrude Stein and Alice B. Toklas were guests here in 1935 and Herb Caen was beaten up twice in the Mark Hopkins around 1940.

Continue along California Street to the:

8. **Stanford Court Hotel,** which incorporates one of the walls of the original Stanford Mansion. Leland Stanford, who was both governor of and U.S. Senator from California, studied law in an Albany, New York, office and was admitted to the Bar in 1848. He married a local Albany girl by the name of Jane Lathrop, and together they went West—first to Wisconsin and then to California, where they built

their fortune together. He orchestrated the building of the Central (later Southern) Pacific Railroad, and their marriage was actually quite harmonious. However, in 1884 tragedy struck when they lost their son to typhoid fever in Florence. Stanford told his wife, "The children of California shall be our children."

Together, in 1886, they endowed Leland Stanford Junior University (still the legal name) in Palo Alto at the estate near San Francisco they had purchased from George Gordon. The university opened in 1891, but the endowment was threatened later by a growing national panic. In 1893, during his effort to keep his university alive, Leland died. Jane continued his work, living frugally, selling off property, and driving around in a 30-year-old car to save money to support the university. She died in 1905. Today Stanford University consistently ranks among the finest institutions of higher learning in the United States.

If you're at all interested in hotel decor, do go in and take a look because the outside of the building is deceptively plain.

Cross to the other side of California Street and retrace your steps to the corner of California and Mason streets opposite the Mark Hopkins Hotel. You're now standing alongside the elegantly white, neo-baroque:

9. **Fairmont Hotel,** which was built by Tessie Fair Oelrichs, the daughter of silver magnate James G. Fair. Fair, born in Ireland in 1831, came to the West for the Gold Rush in 1849. He was one of the original founders and developers of the Comstock Lode but, because of the break-up of his marriage, never built a mansion on Nob Hill like the rest of the Bonanza Kings.

The decision to dynamite various sections of the city during the 1906 fire was made in the ballroom here and announced by General Frederick Funston. After the fire, the badly damaged hotel was restored by the architect Julia Morgan.

Go inside the hotel to view the immense Empire red and gold gilt lobby and to ride in the glass elevators to the top floor, where you'll be treated to a spectacular view. The Fairmont's Venetian Room is a renowned San Francisco supper club.

When you exit the hotel, go right to the intersection of Mason and Sacramento streets, where the horizon (on both sides) opens to a dramatic vista. Go left on Sacramento, staying to the left side of the street, so that you can get a good view of three notable:

10. Sacramento Street homes on the right side of the street. The first, at 1172 Sacramento Street, is a remarkable town house constructed in 1908. If you continue on Sacramento across Taylor Street you'll find 1230 and 1242 Sacramento Street (also on the right side). These two homes are probably the most aesthetically pleasing of the buildings on this street (even though they exist in the shadow of the big hotels). Both are reminiscent of Parisian architecture with their bay windows and cast-iron balconies. Note the plaster detailing.

As you continue along towards Leavenworth Street you'll also come across two beautifully maintained alleyways. Look first on your left for Leroy Place, and then look for Golden Court on the same side of the street, just a little farther on.

When you reach Leavenworth Street, you'll see:

11. The San Loretto Apartments, straight ahead of you on the southwest corner of Leavenworth. Here, in apartment 2 at 1155 Leavenworth Street, was Dashiell Hammett's final address in San Francisco and it is where he finished his novel, *The Maltese Falcon.*

Go right up Leavenworth Street to Clay Street. You are now at the highest point of Nob Hill. If you look to your right along Clay Street you'll be able to see the Transamerica Pyramid.

Continue along Leavenworth Street to Washington Street. Go right, passing Jones and Taylor streets, to Mason Street. On your left side is the:

12. Cable Car Barn and Power House. This fascinating "museum" is your last stop on the Nob Hill walking tour, so take your time.

Probably more famous than the Transamerica Pyramid or any other landmark in San Francisco is the city's cable car system, and the whole thing is run out of this building. The cable car system was invented by Andrew Hallidie, a metal rope manufacturer from Scotland. Hallidie got the idea for the cable car system when he saw a horse and carriage tumble backwards down a hill because the hill was too steep and the carriage's load too heavy.

The original line only ran from Clay Street down Nob Hill, but the system grew. (Leland Stanford is responsible for the California Street line because he wanted to be delivered to his front door every evening.) As the cable car system grew, areas of the city that had previously been inaccessible by horse and wagon (and just too steep for people to climb) were developed.

Before the 1906 earthquake and fire the cable car system was running 600 different cars, but it too suffered great damage during that disaster. After the quake, the system was never the same again.

Today the system runs only three lines, which underwent a $60-million restoration project in 1984. They've been registered as a National Historic Landmark since 1964, and they are here to stay.

Go inside the Cable Car Barn, first to the underground viewing room where you can see each of the single cables that runs the cable cars. There are brief written explanations outside each area so you can really get a grip on what you're looking at. The museum has a gift shop that sells books, postcards, and various cable-car reproductions.

Your tour ends here, but if you're ready for lunch, there's a nice little eatery located on Taylor Street. From the Cable Car Barn go right on Mason to Clay Street. Go right again on Clay, then left on Taylor Street (yes, you'll be ready to sit down by the time you get there).

Winding Down **The Nob Hill Café** is a very small and extremely popular place, so you might have to wait for a few minutes, but the food is excellent and not too expensive. Try one of their individual size pizzas and the minestrone soup.

If you're going to couple this tour with the Russian Hill tour, go back to the intersection of Taylor and Clay streets and continue along Taylor (if you're skipping lunch and starting directly from the museum, go left on Taylor Street) to Broadway.

RUSSIAN HILL

Start: Corner of Broadway and Taylor Street (at the top of the steps).

Public Transportation: The 83 bus will take you within a block of where you want to be.

Finish: Corner of Chestnut and Jones streets.

Time: 2 hours.

Best Times: Tuesday through Saturday between 10am and 5pm.

Worst Times: Monday and Sunday when the San Francisco Art Institute is closed.

Hills That Could Kill: The steps that lead to the upper level of Broadway from Taylor Street, but there's no way to avoid them unless you take a cab.

Local legend has it that Russian Hill's name is a memento of the visits that groups of Russian seamen, who came down from Sitka to hunt sea otter for their skins, made. Those who died on the expeditions apparently were buried on this hill.

Russian Hill was a bohemian center long before Telegraph Hill or North Beach, and while the millionaires were busy sprucing up Nob Hill with mansions, the artists and writers of

Russian Hill were living in little shacks and cottages, painting the views, drinking cheap wine, and taking part in intellectual discourse. Today there's still a small community of writers and artists on the hill, but for the most part they've all been driven to other neighborhoods (such as the Mission District) by rising rents.

This tour will take you by the homes and haunts of famous bohemians like Ina Donna Coolbrith and Jack Kerouac. You'll also get a feel for the local color as you pass the homes of Kate Atkinson and Pop Demarest. You'll discover hidden passages with wooden steps and you'll be charmed by the cottage-style homes at the hill's summit. And, of course, there are the views.

• • • • • • • • • • • • • • • • •

Begin at the corner of Broadway and Taylor Street. Proceed up the Broadway steps. Your first stop will be at the top:

1032 Broadway, the former home of Kate Atkinson, who for many years opened her doors to various artists and writers. A group of writers called "Les Jeunes" were among those who gathered here. Nine young, irreverent members made up the group, but by far the most interesting of them was Gelett Burgess.

Burgess, born in Boston in 1868, received a B.S. from the Massachusetts Institute of Technology before moving to San Francisco, where he worked for Southern Pacific Railway and for the University of California.

He made a speedy entrance into the literary world as an editor of a weekly publication called the *Wave,* where he replaced Frank Norris (who had left to complete *McTeague*). It didn't take long for Burgess to found his own publication, the *Lark.*

Working with the other members of Les Jeunes, Burgess printed the *Lark* on bamboo paper and filled its pages with whatever struck his fancy. Each issue featured a serious poem, essay, and fictional story, but most of its pages were filled with nonsensical rhyming verse. One of the ditties you'll no doubt recognize was written by Burgess himself:

> *I never Saw a Purple Cow;*
> *I never Hope to See One;*
> *But I can Tell you, Anyhow,*
> *I'd rather See than Be one.*

After its publication in one of the 24 issues of the *Lark* (plus an *Epilark*), the country went mad for it, and it was published and quoted and requoted in thousands of magazines. Everybody knew about the "Purple Cow," including Theodore Roosevelt who used to yell out "Purple Cow" every time he saw Burgess.

Needless to say, the poor man was driven crazy by this unwanted notoriety and he even went so far as to print a sort of retraction in the last edition of the magazine:

> *Ah, yes, I Wrote the "Purple Cow"—*
> *I'm sorry, now, I Wrote it!*
> *But I can Tell you Anyhow,*
> *I'll Kill you if you Quote it.*

Burgess also wrote a wonderful poem entitled "The Ballad of the Hyde Street Grip," for which he would probably rather be remembered, so we'll leave one of his favorite hangouts with a stanza from that rhyme:

> *North Beach to Tenderloin, over Russian Hill,*
> *The grades are something giddy, and the curves*
> *   are fit to kill!*
> *All the way to Market Street, clanging up the slope,*
> *Down upon the other side, clinging to the rope!*
> *But the view of San Francisco, as you take the*
> *   lurching dip!*
> *There is plenty of excitement on the Hyde Street*
> *   Grip!*

Directly across the street is:

2. **1051 Broadway,** one of Herb Gold's residences. Gold, a former student at New York's Columbia University and classmate of Allen Ginsberg, has lived in San Francisco for over 30 years. He's a best-selling author and his novels include *Fathers* and *Dreaming*. He contributes regularly to magazines, and is well-known for his witty essays about

Russian Hill

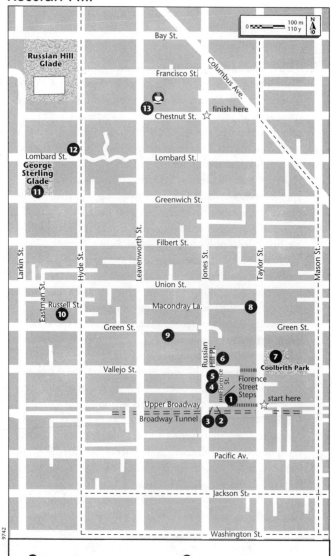

1 1032 Broadway	**8** Macondray Lane
2 1051 Broadway	**9** 1067 Green Street
3 1067 Broadway	**10** 29 Russell Street
4 Demarest Compound	**11** George Sterling Glade
5 40-42 Florence Street	**12** former home of Robert
6 Russian Hill Place	Louis Stevenson's wife
7 Ina Coolbrith Park	**13** San Francisco Art Institute

San Francisco. One of his recent volumes of essays is *Travels in San Francisco.*

A bit farther on is:

3. **1067 Broadway,** the former home of poet Ina Donna Coolbrith (1842–1928). The niece of Mormon Church founder Joseph Smith, she was born Josephine Smith, the daughter of Joseph's brother, Don Carlos. Coolbrith's father died when she was only four months old, and her mother, who abandoned Mormonism because she disagreed with polygamy, took Josephine and her two siblings from Nauvoo, Illinois, west to St. Louis. They finally took the epic journey overland to California, stopping first in San Francisco, but finally settling in Los Angeles.

Josephine began writing, and at the age of 11, she had her first poems published in the *Los Angeles Star.* At 17 she married Robert B. Carsley, a minstrel show performer. Three short and brutal years later she divorced him and moved to San Francisco, taking the name Ina Donna Coolbrith, under which she had been writing her poetry.

Besides being a poet she was an inspiration for writers, poets, artists, and philosophers in early San Francisco and was greatly loved by her contemporaries.

She began working with Bret Harte on the *Overland Monthly* (in 1868), but poetry did not pay her bills or support her family, so she took a job in the Oakland Public Library where she worked for over 25 years. It was in the Oakland library that she met 12-year-old Jack London, who was poor, shabbily dressed, and generally uncared for. He was asking for something to read. Coolbrith guided and inspired him, and of her he said, "I loved Ina Coolbrith above all womankind, and what I am and what I have done that is good I owe to her."

In 1915 at the age of 73 she was proclaimed Poet Laureate of California at the University of California.

Head up the set of stairs on the right side of the road (the Florence Street Steps) to Florence Street. Before you get to the top, you'll see a wooden gate. It used to be the way to get to the:

4. **Demarest Compound,** at 1078–80 Broadway. The old "compound" was really just a small grouping of cottages

that was built to house refugees after the earthquake of 1906. After the refugees moved, the cottages, surrounded by shrubs and flowers, were home to many writers, but they no longer exist. However, you can't take a trip to Russian Hill without learning about old Pop Demarest, who built the cottages and owned the land upon which they were built.

Pop Demarest lived up here until he died in 1939 at the age of 87, but he wasn't known to more than a handful of people until his obituary, which called him "The Hermit of Russian Hill," was published. For many years he lived in an abandoned cistern pipe under the buildings at the Compound, later moving into the basement of one of the cottages.

Demarest hated to bathe, but he loved to drink, and every month he would go on a drunken binge. For several days he would run naked through the Compound gardens, throwing bottles and making a general nuisance of himself. His tenants didn't mind, though; they just locked their doors and waited patiently until he quieted down. His tenants were probably tolerant of this outrageous behavior—in part, at least—because Demarest didn't really care when or if they paid their rent. Money meant nothing to him.

After he died, reporters flocked to his basement room to see what it was like. They found it full of cobwebs, knick-knacks, dried animal skins, thousands of records (many by Adelina Patti, whom he was crazy about), photographs, and hordes of hungry cats.

When you reach the top of the stairs you'll be on Florence Street. Look for:

5. **40–42 Florence Street,** which was once the home of architect Willis Polk (1867–1924). In his early career, Polk spent time working for the firm Van Brunt and Howe in Kansas City, later for A. Page Brown in New York. When Brown moved his office to San Francisco in 1889, Polk moved with him, and it was here that Polk flourished. His work has been described as "versatile" and "unpredictable," paving the way for many San Francisco architects to come. The tendency to mix and match styles is a technique frequently repeated in San Francisco homes of the Victorian period. Polk built an enormous number of houses and

worked on many churches and office buildings during his career. In 1917 he designed the first glass curtain-walled building in the world (the Hallidie Building at 130–150 Sutter Street).

While he made his living in architecture, Polk still had time to take part in some bohemian escapades. In fact, he was an active member of Les Jeunes and often contributed drawings or architectural essays to some of the magazines of the time, like Gelett Burgess's *Lark.*

Go on around and take in the view from the end of Florence Street then return to the Florence Street Steps continuing up. At the top, cross Florence Street, heading into:

6. Russian Hill Place. Mystery writer Virginia Rath, once a resident of Russian Hill Place, gave one of her characters, Michael Dundas, a home here in the quaint, hidden cul-de-sac that tops Russian Hill.

Born in Colusa County, California, Rath had her primary education in country schools, where she began writing and submitting stories to publishers before she was 16. She attended the University of California and became a teacher. Instead of taking a planned trip to Europe, she married Carl Rath settling in Portola for another five years.

Her first novel, *Death at Dagton's Folly,* was published in 1935 by the Crime Club. Her next few novels made her one of the most popular mystery writers of her time.

Come back out of Russian Hill Place and go left to the end of Vallejo Street, where you'll find a set of stairs. Go down the stairs, cross Taylor Street, and follow another set of stairs into:

7. Ina Coolbrith Park. Coolbrith lived near here on Taylor Street until her apartment burned down in the fire of 1906.

In the fire she lost letters from friends like Lord Tennyson, Dante Gabriel Rossetti, Henry Wadsworth Longfellow, and closer everyday friends like Mark Twain, Bret Harte, and Charles Warren Stoddard. She met Twain and Stoddard when she worked in the offices of the *Overland Monthly,* of which Bret Harte was editor.

Harte, Stoddard, and Coolbrith enjoyed taking trips to Mount Tamalpais and Muir Woods, and they often drank together in Sausalito or sat in her Russian Hill house reading poetry together.

After the fire destroyed her home her, friends raised money and purchased two apartments for her, one of which provided enough rental income to meet her living expenses.

Come out of the park the way you entered, and go right on Taylor Street until you come to:

8. **Macondray Lane,** the quintessential San Francisco pedestrian street, inaccessible to cars or any other form of transportation. Some people believe that this street was the model for Armistead Maupin's Barbary Lane, while others believe Filbert Street was, because of its proximity to Maupin's own home.

In any case, it's a wonderful street to walk along, with its overhanging trees and wandering flowers. You're sure to find several cats hanging out under the steps or near the houses.

When you come to Jones Street, go left to Green Street. Go right on Green Street to:

9. **1067 Green Street,** which will be on your left. This octagonal house, better known as the Feusier Octagon, was originally constructed in 1859. Louis Feusier, a San Francisco merchant, added the cupola and mansard roofing 20 or 30 years later.

A bit farther along, on the right, is a Tudor Revival firehouse (No. 31) that dates from 1907 and was designed by Newton J. Tharp. The firehouse was still in use until the early 1950s. It was later purchased and restored by Louise S. Davies, who donated it to the National Trust for Historic Preservation in 1978.

Continue along Green Street to Hyde Street. Go right on Hyde to Russell Street. Go left to:

10. **29 Russell Street,** where Jack Kerouac lived with Neal Cassady and Neal's wife when he came back to the West Coast in 1952. During his six-month stay, Kerouac worked on revising *On the Road* and collaborated with Cassady on the art of spontaneous writing. Out of some of their conversations (which were tape recorded as examples of spontaneity) came several sections of *Visions of Cody.*

If you continue west on Russell Street, you'll come to the intersection of Eastman Street. Go right here to Union

Street, and then go left. When you get to Larkin Street, go right to the Greenwich Street Steps that will take you up to:

11. **George Sterling Glade.** Go up the ramp by the tennis courts to get into the park.

After the suicide of the "King of Bohemia," George Sterling's friends and contemporaries gathered for the dedication of this memorial park. A tiled bench and plaque were installed here, but the bench broke and the plaque was stolen, so in 1982 another dedication was made and a new plaque was installed. Engraved on the plaque are Sterling's own words about San Francisco:

> *Tho the dark be cold and blind,*
> *Yet her sea-fog's touch is kind,*
> *And her mightier caress,*
> *Is joy and the pain thereof:*
> *And great is thy tenderness,*
> *O cool, gray city of love!*

Come back out of the park and go left to Hyde Street. Go left on Hyde Street to Lombard Street. Before heading down Lombard Street, note that on the northwest corner of Lombard and Hyde is the:

12. **former home of Robert Louis Stevenson's wife,** where for years many people believed Stevenson himself resided, but he never did. After Stevenson died, his wife came back to San Francisco and commissioned this house. It's a Willis Polk design.

Now go right down Lombard Street, the "Crookedest Street in the World," and probably the most heavily touristed street in all of San Francisco. It was built this way in the 1920s to make it easier to traverse because of its steep grades.

At the end of Lombard go left on Leavenworth Street to Chestnut Street. Go right to the:

13. **San Francisco Art Institute,** at 800 Chestnut Street. Founded in 1871, it's the oldest art school in the West. There are three art galleries inside. The Diego Rivera Gallery displays student work in addition to the 1931 Rivera mural on the right as you enter. In addition, there's a photography gallery and a professional gallery.

Some people think that the Art Institute's tower is haunted, but that doesn't seem to bother the students who work here.

Winding Down   You're at the end of the tour now and you're probably ready for a refreshment stop. The Institute's cafe is located at the back of the building.

FISHERMAN'S WHARF

Start: Corner of Bay and Laguna streets.

Public Transportation: 28 bus to Bay and Laguna streets.

Finish: Pier 19.

Time: 2 hours, not including museum stops.

Best Times: After 10am when shops and museums are open.

Worst Times: Before 10am.

Hills That Could Kill: None.

Before you start your tour of Fisherman's Wharf you should know about the man who is responsible for its initial development. Harry Meiggs was so well liked by city residents that he was called "Honest" Harry Meiggs all over San Francisco. As it turned out, though, the charming, generous, and handsome gentleman was a dreamer, and a schemer, a scoundrel, and a thief.

Born in New York State, Harry Meiggs spent his youth buying and selling lumber, but after news of the discovery of gold in California reached him he headed West, arriving in San Francisco in July 1849.

He established a lumber business in North Beach, building a sawmill and a small wharf to which he ferried lumber from a larger sawmill in Mendocino County. That year he also became a city alderman, but his great dream was to develop North Beach, which was far removed from the city in those days. Meiggs contended that it made more sense for development of the city to spread to the north, rather than south to Market Street, as the city had been doing. He proposed a wharf at the end of Powell Street. Boats could anchor right at North Beach instead of being pulled around Telegraph Hill by tugboats, which was the usual practice at that time.

But Meiggs became sidetracked with other projects and the development of the wharf was delayed. First, he helped George Gordon develop South Park, the elegant haven for San Francisco's elite at the foot of Rincon Hill. He also helped Rudolph Herold (a pianist who studied with Mendelssohn) to establish the Philharmonic Society of San Francisco. But Meiggs didn't abandon his dream.

First, he laid down a road that ran from Montgomery Street to North Beach and then he built his wharf extending 2,000 feet out into the bay, at Powell Street. He then began developing North Beach in earnest, but it was an enormous expense and made him very cash-poor. In 1854, when depression hit San Francisco for the first time, property values crashed, and Meiggs was forced into bankruptcy, a fact that he kept secret from all who knew him.

As an alderman he was respected as a trustworthy member of society, which enabled him, without being questioned, to forge the signatures of mayors and controllers on promissory notes to pay his debts. He later forged notes of private corporations and San Francisco merchants—including fraudulent notes of his own lumber company.

Before anyone realized what he had been doing, Meiggs chartered the brig *American* and on the morning of October 6, 1854, he set sail for Tahiti and Chile. He later settled in Peru, where he made his fortune building railroads all over South America.

In 1873 a bill passed the legislature pardoning Meiggs, but it was vetoed by the governor. He died in Peru in 1877, having left his heart in San Francisco.

After Meiggs left, trade at the wharf grew, and a thriving fishing industry developed. The first to use the wharf were the Chinese; the Italians followed, forcing the Chinese out of business. In fact, the Italians became so strongly associated with Fisherman's Wharf that few people even remember that the Chinese were there at all.

The colorful Italian fishing fleet would set sail every day to bring back the catch that supplied the wharf's primarily Italian restaurants (and the rest of the city) with fresh fish and crabs. Fishing in the bay continued for many years, but after World War II the fish population in the bay was severely diminished, and the fishing fleets had to go farther afield.

There are still a few fishermen making their living at Fisherman's Wharf today, but most of the wharf's revenue comes from an active tourist trade. However, in spite of the tourist shops that have taken over the waterfront, you can still get fresh seafood, and of course, the views are spectacular. If you come early in the morning, you can see the fish being unloaded and the fog lifting gently off the bay—then you can really understand Harry Meiggs's original dream.

• • • • • • • • • • • • • • • •

Follow Laguna Street in the direction of the water, go straight down to the corner of Beach and Laguna streets, and then right towards the water and piers. You're now heading into the:

1. **Fort Mason Cultural Center,** which was established as a headquarters for the U.S. Army during the Westward Expansion. After the fire and earthquake of 1906 tents were set up here as temporary shelter for refugees. In fact, Ina Donna Coolbrith was one who called the tent-dotted military grounds home after her apartment burned (see Walking Tour 6, stop 7 for details). Fort Mason also served as a significant military base during World War II.

Today, in the same buildings (in front of you) that were used as army offices and barracks, you'll find several interesting museums. The first is the San Francisco Craft and Folk Art Museum, located in Building A, where you'll be able to explore exhibits of folk arts and crafts from all over the world.

Fisherman's Wharf

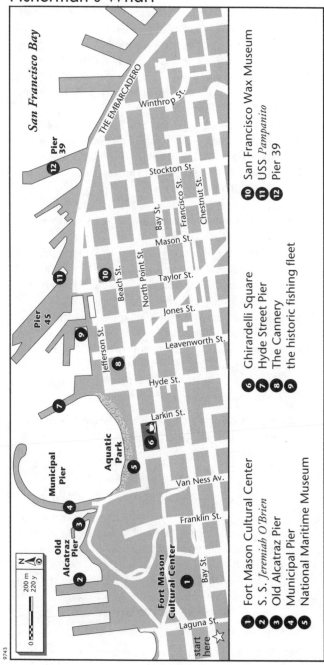

San Francisco Bay

THE EMBARCADERO

Winthrop St.

Stockton St.

Bay St.

Francisco St.

Chestnut St.

Mason St.

North Point St.

Beach St.

Taylor St.

Jones St.

Leavenworth St.

Jefferson St.

Hyde St.

Larkin St.

Van Ness Av.

Franklin St.

Bay St.

Laguna St.

Pier 39

Pier 45

Municipal Pier

Aquatic Park

Old Alcatraz Pier

Fort Mason Cultural Center

start here

0 200 m
   220 y

N

9743

1 Fort Mason Cultural Center	**6** Ghirardelli Square
2 S. S. *Jeremiah O'Brien*	**7** Hyde Street Pier
3 Old Alcatraz Pier	**8** The Cannery
4 Municipal Pier	**9** the historic fishing fleet
5 National Maritime Museum	
10 San Francisco Wax Museum	
11 USS *Pampanito*	
12 Pier 39	

Next door, while it's probably too soon for a refreshment stop, you'll be happy to find Green's, San Francisco's best vegetarian restaurant. It's run by the Marin Zen Center, and its opening in 1979 brought new meaning to vegetarian cuisine. As you can imagine, this establishment also offers an excellent view of the bay and the famous Golden Gate Bridge.

Also in Building A is the San Francisco Museum of Modern Art Rental Gallery, part of the San Francisco Museum of Modern Art. You will find exhibitions of works by contemporary artists here. If you're interested, you can either buy or rent these pieces.

In Building C you'll find the Museo Italo Americano, where exhibitions of works by contemporary Italian or Italian American artists are held.

The Mexican Museum is located in Building D, and you can view the works of Mexican artists here for a small admission charge. Also in Building D is the Magic Theater, founded in 1967, whose resident troupe is best known for putting on the plays of little-known, controversial, or emerging playwrights. Sam Shepard's Pulitzer Prize–winner *Buried Child* premiered here, and over the last 12 years he has consistently premiered his plays here.

When you come out of the converted warehouses, go toward the water to Pier 3, where you'll find the:

2. **S.S. Jeremiah O'Brien,** the last surviving Liberty Ship of the 2,751 that were launched between 1941 and 1945.

This particular ship was built and originally launched from Portland, Maine, in 1943, but it is similar to those that were launched from the Bay Area. It was constructed in only 56 days and was part of the fleet that carried supplies to Allied forces. Shortly after D-Day it landed on the French coast, making several more runs across the Atlantic before the end of the war in Europe. It was later moved to the Pacific, which is how it ended up here.

Registered as a National Historic Landmark, the *O'Brien* is open daily for tours from 9am to 3pm.

Follow the path along with the bay on your left. Just at the bottom of the hill you'll find the:

3. **Old Alcatraz Pier** to your left. It's closed to the public now, but it was on this pier that prisoners were held before

being transported to "The Rock," as Alcatraz is known, until the closing of the prison in 1963.

Writer Barnaby Conrad once had a studio in one of the old holding cells here. Conrad was one of the many who gave San Francisco its local color. As Herb Caen described him, Conrad was the local bullfighting expert, San Francisco's own Hemingway. In the 1950s Conrad even opened a restaurant in North Beach called El Matador. He wrote hundreds of articles and a few novels about bullfighting, and some people said that even though San Francisco never played host to any bullfights city residents knew more about bullfighting than anyone else in the country, thanks to Barnaby Conrad.

Alcatraz

Alcatraz Island got its name when an English sea captain drew a map of the area and mistakenly labeled the island "Isla de Alcatraces" (Pelican Island), the name that was originally given to Yerba Buena Island by the Spanish. Commonly referred to as "The Rock," Alcatraz was originally used in the 1850s as a military post to protect the bay from outside attacks. From the late 1850s until 1907 Alcatraz was also used as a military prison, and after the fort closed, the military prison remained until 1933. The next year the Army vacated the island entirely, and Alcatraz became a federal maximum-security prison from which there was no escape. Prison authorities thought that if a prisoner actually managed to get beyond the wall of the compound he would never make it down the jagged cliff walls. Even if he did that, it would be impossible for him to swim from the island to the mainland. In fact, while several prisoners attempted to escape from Alcatraz, only one may have succeeded.

Some of Alcatraz's more notorious inmates were "Machine Gun" Kelly, Al Capone, and Robert Stroud, "The Birdman of Alcatraz." All the prisoners were removed from Alcatraz in 1963 after Robert Kennedy (then Attorney General) and a congressional committee decided that continuing to maintain prisoners there was too expensive.

The long arm of a pier that you see stretching out before you just beyond the Old Alcatraz Pier is the:

4. **Municipal Pier.** Take a walk to the end of the 1,850-foot pier so you can admire the view. Note as you walk that this pier and the area to your right is Aquatic Park, which was built between 1929 and 1934; the small beach along the shoreline was created for joggers and swimmers. Unfortunately, the water is so cold during most of the year that any swimmers you see are likely to be members of the Polar Bear Club.

   Fishing is permitted at the end of the Municipal Pier, so while you're down here, you might spot some sport fishermen dropping their lines.

   After you've finished admiring the view, head back to shore and go left. Follow the path and you'll find yourself outside the art deco:

5. **National Maritime Museum.** Shaped like a ship with portholes and all, this museum is filled with sailing, whaling, and fishing lore. You'll find a great collection of scrimshaw and shipwreck photos. There's even an 1851 photograph of the hundreds of abandoned ships left en masse by crews hurrying off to participate in the Gold Rush.

   The museum's walls are lined with ornately carved and painted figureheads from old ships. Inside you'll find a model of the *Preussen*, the largest sailing vessel ever built.

   Cross Beach Street after leaving the Maritime Museum and go left to:

6. **Ghirardelli Square.** Domingo Ghirardelli, founder of the chocolate company, was born in Rapallo, Italy, in 1817, and as a boy he apprenticed himself to a confectioner. He later moved to Peru and opened his own candy shop. During his time there he had occasion to meet one of San Francisco's best, a man by the name of James Lick. Lick so enjoyed Ghirardelli's chocolate that he personally carried over 600 pounds of it back to San Francisco.

   In 1849, when Ghirardelli moved to San Francisco, he dazzled the taste buds of its residents, and while others were busy mining gold, he was making his fortune in chocolate. He later expanded his business to include the marketing of spices.

The shopping center you see today was the original Ghiradelli chocolate factory, built between 1900 and 1916. The sign that crowns the top has been there since it opened. The "Mermaid Fountain" at the center of the complex was designed by Ruth Asawa.

Spend some time browsing through the shops here. You'll find clothing boutiques, jewelry shops, toy stores, and folk art shops, as well as several restaurants.

Take a Break A great restaurant in Ghirardelli Square is **Mandarin,** with its exposed beam-and-twig ceilings and silk-covered walls. It serves exceptional Chinese cuisine; I especially recommend the Szechuan string beans.

Also in Ghirardelli Square is **Gaylord's, a** fine Indian restaurant, serving North Indian haute cuisine. It's fairly expensive, but worth it.

Head out of Ghirardelli Square via Beach Street and cross through Victorian Park to the corner of Jefferson and Hyde streets. Go left on Hyde to the:

7. **Hyde Street Pier,** where you'll find several historic ships. Look for the *Balclutha,* a three-masted square-rigger that was built in Scotland in 1886. It was used to carry grain and coal (among other things) from California and could travel at a clip of 300 miles a day. In its lifetime, it rounded Cape Horn 17 times and even survived a near wreck off the coast of Alaska in 1906. During the last 30 years the *Balclutha* was in service it made trips to Alaska for canned salmon. In 1934 the *Balclutha* played a minor role in the movie *Mutiny on the Bounty.*

The *C. A. Thayer,* a three-masted schooner, built in 1895, was constructed for the lumber trade and carried logs from the Pacific Northwest to the many carpentry shops of California.

The *Eureka,* an 1890 paddle-wheel ferry, made its final trip in 1957. It's a side-wheeler that used to carry cars as well as passengers, and if you go on deck you'll find that it's loaded with a cargo that includes antique cars and trucks.

The *Wapama,* originally built in 1915, is an exemplary product of the Industrial Revolution because it began as a sailing vessel but was later fitted with a steam engine.

Other ships here include the two-masted *Alma; Hercules,* an oceangoing steam tug built in 1907; and *Eppleton Hall,* an English side-wheeled tugboat constructed in 1914 and originally meant to operate on the Thames River.

Come off the pier and go left on Jefferson Street to:

8. **The Cannery,** which was built at the turn of the century as a peach-canning plant for the Del Monte Fruit Company. Like Ghirardelli Square, it was remodeled as a shopping center in the late 1960s.

The red brick exterior was left intact, while the interior was transformed into a shopping and entertainment complex. During the summer live entertainment is held here in the courtyard, set in the midst of a grove of olive trees over 100 years old.

Within the complex on the second floor is the San Francisco International Toy Museum, where you can amuse yourself with the rotating collection of old toys. A relatively new addition, the Museum of the History of San Francisco (opened in 1991), is located on the third floor of the complex, and although exhibits must be rotated for of lack of space, the museum's curators are eventually hoping to acquire more collections and expand into a larger space.

Come out of the Cannery and go right along Jefferson, crossing Leavenworth Street, for about a block. Cross to the other side of Jefferson, and you'll be standing in front of:

9. **the historic fishing fleet,** some of which bring in a daily catch at about 5am or 6am every morning. If you're up at that hour you can watch them unloading. More than likely you'll be here long after the fleet is in, but there's still plenty to see later in the day, like the seals and sea lions that hang out hoping for a snack. They only eat fish and they'll bark at you if you look like a softhearted soul.

Go left off Jefferson Street and follow the wooden pier around. Feel free to wander the wharves. At the end of Pier 49 you'll find a small wood "shack" that actually serves as the fishermen's chapel—it even has one stained-glass window.

This is the heart of Fisherman's Wharf, and was once the center of the city's commercial fishing business although you'd never be able to tell now because of the cheap souvenir shops and amusement park atmosphere. When the wharf was at its most active over 300 ships docked here. But of the ones you see here today, only about half of them set out on fishing expeditions all year round. Currently the fishing fleet that lands here only supplies a fraction of the fish for the restaurants and shops around the city.

Note: If you're interested in coming back early some morning to catch a glimpse of the fishing fleet unloading their catch, you should go down Fish Alley, which is located between Jones and Hyde streets just off Jefferson Street.

Go back out to Jefferson Street and continue to the left.

Take a Break   You should stop in at the **Boudin** (pronounced "bo-deen" by San Franciscans) **Sourdough French Bread Bakery** at 156 Jefferson Street, a distant relative to San Francisco's first bakery, which was opened in 1849 on Grant Avenue by Isadore Boudin.

They bake great sourdough bread and decadent chocolate croissants—you'll never find another croissant with as much chocolate filling as you will here. You can also enjoy soup and other light snacks.

Across the street is the:

10. **San Francisco Wax Museum** at 145 Jefferson Street. The museum holds nearly 300 extraordinary models of famous people. Those who enjoy this type of museum will find wax figures of characters such as Nikita Khrushchev, Michael Jackson, and George Bush. Who could resist a look around in the Chamber of Horrors, where you'll find Dracula and Frankenstein?

If you decide to pass up the wax museum, just turn left on Taylor Street and past the parking area onto Pier 45 where you'll find (on the right side of the pier) the:

11. **U.S.S. Pampanito,** a battle-scarred World War II submarine that saw a great deal of action in the Pacific. Built in 1943 in Portland, Maine, the *Pampanito,* which can dive 600 feet below the surface, is responsible for having sunk five Japanese ships.

You can tour the submarine, but if you're claustrophobic I wouldn't recommend it—quarters are very close. If you do go inside, you can take a self-guided audio tour for a small admission fee. Imagine how cramped it must have been for the naval officers and crew who manned this ship!

You'll also notice that some fishing boats still unload on this pier daily.

If you're hungry when you come back off the pier, continue straight back onto Taylor Street.

☕ Winding Down   At 2766 Taylor Street, on the third floor, you'll find an Italian seafood restaurant just like the ones that used to line the wharf back in the mid-1800s. **A. Sabella** has been here since 1920 and serves a variety of creative local seafood dishes as well as pasta.

Head back to the entrance of Pier 45 and go right along the Embarcadero. As you pass Pier 43 and Pier 41 note that you can catch ferries to Angel and Alcatraz islands, respectively, from here.

Your final stop on this tour is at:

12. **Pier 39,** the entrance to which is at Embarcadero and Beach streets. Another heavily touristed area, these buildings make up a two-level shopping street that is supposed to be a replica of a turn-of-the-century San Francisco street, but it seems incredibly out of place. It looks more like something you'd find on Cape Cod.

However, if you feel like shopping for some more souvenirs—T-shirts and things—this is the place. You can also grab an inexpensive snack at one of the take-out places.

If you're not interested in shopping, window shopping, or eating, I would recommend at least walking to the end of the pier (which used to be a cargo pier) simply to get a look at the spectacular view. You'll probably also want to watch the frolicking sea lions who have taken up residence here.

PACIFIC HEIGHTS

Start: Corner of Washington and Laguna streets.

Public Transportation: Take the 12 bus to the corner of Washington and Laguna streets.

Finish: Corner of Union and Gough streets.

Time: 3 hours, not including shopping stops.

Best Times: Wednesdays, in the early afternoon, when the Haas-Lilienthal House and the stores are open.

Worst Times: Outside normal shopping hours.

Hills That Could Kill: Octavia Street between Pacific and Washington streets.

After the cable car line through Pacific Heights was built in 1878, the neighborhood evolved in much the same way as Nob Hill. Vistas were expensive, and only San Francisco's wealthiest could afford to build homes here. Over time Pacific Heights has become one of San Francisco's most highbrow neighborhoods. As you walk along this tour, you'll find more mansions per block than anywhere else in the city. I've highlighted some of them—mostly ones with a story behind them, but there are plenty of others to look at as you walk.

• • • • • • • • • • • • • • •

From the corner of Washington and Laguna streets, look for Lafayette Park (which you will visit later), and head toward it, just a few steps along Washington to the:

1. **Mary Phelan Mansion,** at 2150 Washington Street. James D. Phelan was Mayor of San Francisco from 1894 to 1902 and served as a United States senator from 1915 to 1921. He commissioned the building of this Renaissance Revival mansion in 1915 for his sister Mary because their home had been destroyed in the 1906 earthquake and fire. Neither James nor Mary ever married, and James kept a suite here in his sister's house.

Go back to Laguna Street and turn right. Continue north, and turn right again onto Jackson Street to the:

2. **Whittier Mansion,** at 2090 Jackson Street, the home of the California Historical Society from 1956 to 1991. This impressive stone mansion was built in 1896 for William Frank Whittier, the former director of the utilities company that is now known as Pacific Gas & Electric Company. When architect Edward R. Swain designed this mansion for Whittier, he installed modern technology, including a hydraulic elevator, electric light fixtures, central heat, and steel reinforcement in its brick and Arizona sandstone walls. As a result of Swain's cutting-edge architecture, the mansion withstood the 1906 earthquake and fire.

Unfortunately the mansion is no longer accessible to the public because it's a private residence, but if you were to go inside you would see walls paneled in every kind of wood imaginable, including birch and mahogany.

Some people believe the house to be haunted by the ghost of William Whittier, but others think it's the ghost of his layabout son, Billy. Billy loved to drink, and since the presence is often detected in the basement where there was probably a wine cellar, I'd vote for Billy.

Continue past the Whittier Mansion to Pacific Avenue and go right. On the corner you'll find the:

3. **Ottilie R. Schubert Hall,** at 2099 Pacific Avenue. This magnificent Classical Revival house was originally built for John D. Spreckels, Jr., in 1904. Sugar producer Claus (the "Sugar King") Spreckels came to the United States from Hanover, Germany, settling first in New York City

Pacific Heights

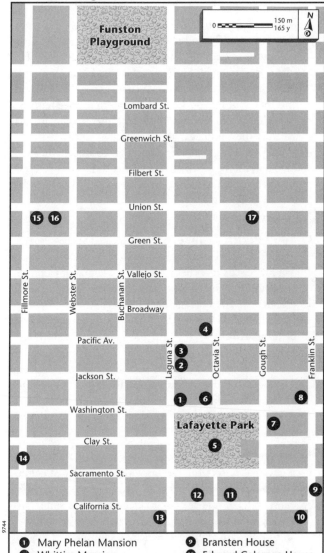

Funston
Playground

0 ——— 150 m
165 y

N

Lombard St.

Greenwich St.

Filbert St.

Union St.

Green St.

Vallejo St.

Broadway

Pacific Av.

Jackson St.

Washington St.

Lafayette Park

Clay St.

Sacramento St.

California St.

Fillmore St.

Webster St.

Buchanan St.

Laguna St.

Octavia St.

Gough St.

Franklin St.

① Mary Phelan Mansion
② Whittier Mansion
③ Ottilie R. Schubert Hall
④ 2000 Pacific Avenue
⑤ Lafayette Park
⑥ Spreckels Mansion
⑦ 2000 Block of Gough Street
⑧ Haas-Lilienthal
   House Museum
⑨ Bransten House
⑩ Edward Coleman House
⑪ 1990 California Street
⑫ 2026 California Street
⑬ 2101 California Street
⑭ Fillmore Street
⑮ 3119 Fillmore Street
⑯ Cow Hollow
⑰ Octagon House

9744

and coming later to San Francisco during the gold rush. After he arrived in San Francisco, Spreckles opened a grocery store and then a brewery. From his profits he started the Bay Sugar Refining Company and became obsessed with sugar, expanding his business to Hawaii. He made Hawaii one of the greatest sugar-producing centers of the world, and then sent his son John to Hawaii to oversee business. While there John Spreckels built a steamer trading line that sailed to the South Seas and Australia.

Currently the building houses an extensive library of materials on the history of California and its characters. It also holds an enormous collection of articles from the *San Francisco Chronicle*.

Continue along Pacific Avenue to:

4. **2000 Pacific Avenue,** which is located at the corner of Octavia Street. This Queen Anne–style home is just one of San Francisco's most beautiful Painted Ladies. It's a private residence, but the current owners donated a preservation easement to the Foundation for San Francisco's Architectural Heritage, which would prevent any future owners from being able to change the structure and facade of the house. Note the colonial tower on the right side of the house, and the beautifully detailed frieze around the top of the house. The medallion that stands alone in the center of the facade on the second floor is also worthy of note.

Go right on Octavia Street back down to Washington Street. Directly ahead of you is:

5. **Lafayette Park,** which, in addition to its beauty, has an interesting history that begins with a man named Samuel Holladay. Holladay was one of San Francisco's earliest residents, and because he couldn't stand the noise and lack of privacy on Montgomery Street, he sought refuge on a nearby hilltop. It wasn't long before he had built himself a house surrounded by a beautiful garden with trees tall enough to keep out the prying stares of passers-by. He remained happy on his hill until much later, when the beautiful views of his neighborhood (then called the Western Addition) helped make it one of the most fashionable places to live.

It was then that the city decreed that no person was allowed to live on two full city blocks, because that would impede the development of the street grid system. Holladay was told he would have to move, but he refused. Soon he became embroiled in a bitter lawsuit with the city and Holladay vowed that he wouldn't cut his hair until he won the suit.

The battle continued for many years and his white hair grew down past his shoulders before a compromise was reached. The city paid Holladay a tidy sum for his land, but instead of cutting the land with a road, the city leveled his house, planted more trees, and added benches, turning the old Holladay place into a public park.

Lafayette Park is also associated with an odd couple—George Davidson, president of the California Academy of Sciences, and James Lick, the quintessential scrooge.

Lick cared nothing for friends, frivolity, or education—the only thing in life he wanted was money, stacks and stacks of it. He arrived in San Francisco in 1847, quickly amassing quite a fortune from real estate. He used some of his fortune to build an elegant hotel, the Lick House, in which he took a room. Being eccentric, however, he didn't choose to live in a beautifully furnished and decorated room; he lived in virtual squalor and could often be seen wandering about town in dirty ragged clothing.

George Davidson, on the other hand, was a cultured and learned man of moderate means who dedicated his life to teaching.

They came together one evening here in Lafayette Park and the only thing between them was a telescope. Davidson introduced Lick to the stars, and Lick fell in love—probably for the first time in his life. In fact, he was so in love with the science of astronomy that he left $700,000 in his will for the building of an observatory on Mt. Hamilton. He also left money to the poor and the elderly, and of course, to the California Academy of Sciences. It was Davidson and the stars that transformed this scrooge and gave his story a happy ending.

Come back out of the park onto Washington Street and look for the:

6. **Spreckels Mansion,** at 2080 Washington Street, once owned by Adolph, another son of Claus Spreckels. Adolph's

wife, Alma de Bretteville Spreckels, was an art student at one time, but she also did some modeling for various San Francisco artists. She was the model for the statue of Victory atop the Dewey monument in Union Square, and she also modeled for portrait photographer Arnold Genthe at age 15.

Alma and Adolph were responsible for the California Palace of the Legion of Honor in Lincoln Park and its collection of Rodins.

Continue on Washington Street. At the corner of Washington and Gough streets, go right and walk along the:

7. **2000 block of Gough Street,** which will take you around the other side of Lafayette Park for a look at some fine Victorian houses, including No. 2004–2010, built in the Queen Anne style in 1889, and the Eastlake–Queen Anne home just a few doors down at No. 2000. It was built in 1889.

Turn around and return along Gough Street to Washington. Go right to Franklin Street. Go left on Franklin to the:

8. **Haas-Lilienthal House Museum,** at 2007 Franklin Street, also the headquarters for The Foundation for San Francisco's Architectural Heritage.

You should definitely make time to visit this house, not only because it is one of the city's most spectacular Queen Anne–style Victorians, but because you'll get a rare glimpse at the history of an old San Francisco family. Alice Haas-Lilienthal, the daughter of the original owners of the house, lived here from 1886 to 1972 and was able to preserve the house and its contents in spite of the ups and downs of the neighborhood. Two years after Alice's death her family donated the house to The Foundation for San Francisco's Architectural Heritage. The foundation offers tours every half hour on Wednesday from noon to 4pm and Sunday from 11am to 4:30pm.

When you exit the house, turn south onto Franklin, continuing past Washington Street:

9. **Bransten House,** at 1735 Franklin Street. Built in 1904, this Georgian Revival house was a wedding gift of the Haas family to their daughter Florine and her new husband,

Edward Bransten, a coffee magnate. After her husband died in 1948, Florine Haas Bransten lived here for nearly 30 years—and presumably hosted her sister Alice, who lived only three blocks away, from time to time.

Continue along to the:

10. **Edward Coleman House,** at 1701 California Street (corner of Franklin Street). Built in 1895, this Queen Anne–style gem currently houses law offices, and even though it once served as a boarding house it was in decent shape when the law partners purchased it. They did a full restoration in 1975.

Note the wonderful round corner tower and the enormous bay windows.

Go right on California Street to:

11. **1990 California Street,** the former home of Dominga de Goni Atherton, mother-in-law of author Gertrude Atherton. After Dominga's husband died in 1880 she moved from her country home into this sprawling mansion and was joined by her son, George, and her daughter-in-law, Gertrude.

Novelist Gertrude Atherton married into this well-to-do family almost by accident. George proposed to her five times before she unwittingly consented, and after they were married she was miserable with him. She described him as being practically illiterate, boring, nagging, and she went so far as to say, "The worst trial I had yet been called upon to endure was having a husband continually on my hands."

George's mother, it seems, agreed wholeheartedly, and between Gertrude's brush-offs and his mother's insults, George was really quite an unhappy man. In an effort to get away from both of them, he decided to take a trip to Chile. He was only out to sea for a couple of days when his kidney ruptured and he died. George's cousin, who was accompanying him, placed his body in a barrel of rum and sent it back to San Francisco.

Gertrude and Dominga Atherton soon began to feel a ghostly presence in the house. Naturally they assumed it was George (although more than likely it was guilt), and not long after his death they moved out.

Other tenants have noticed strange goings-on in the house, and one or two have even seen an apparition hanging about. A séance revealed four presences (Gertrude, George, Dominga, and a woman who once ran a boarding house here).

Continue along California Street to:

12. **2026 California Street.** Located between Octavia and Laguna streets, this Italianate home with its blue, bronze, and white color scheme is a stately addition to this block. Note the Egyptian head above the doorway—it is reflected in the interior in an Egyptian mural above the fireplace.

Continue on to:

13. **2101 California Street** on your left. Gertrude Atherton had an apartment here beginning in 1929 in which (among other places) she held literary functions and salons until she was well into her 80s. A former member of the literary group Les Jeunes, and one of America's first true feminists, Atherton wrote such novels as *The Doomswoman* (1892) and *Black Oxen* (1923), the latter a best-seller. She was one of San Francisco's most important writers, and before her death in 1948 she published one of her most interesting books, *My San Francisco,* which chronicles the history of some of San Francisco's most famous and infamous residents.

Continue on California Street, past Buchanan and Webster streets and turn right onto:

14. **Fillmore Street,** a great shopping street. First, stop and indulge yourself at Sweet Inspiration, on the left side of Fillmore.

Next there's Vivande Porta Via (at No. 2125), which has a mouth-watering assortment of Italian gourmet groceries, plus a great little Italian restaurant that serves homemade pasta. It borders on expensive, so if you're on a budget and thinking about lunch, I'll be recommending some other less expensive places along Fillmore Street. But if you feel like splurging and you can get a table here, by all means do.

A bit farther on is Fillamento (at No. 2185), a great modern housewares store. Even if you're not shopping for anything in particular you'll probably enjoy a quick browse. A couple of doors farther down is a well-stocked bookstore called Browser Books (at No. 2187).

Take a Break There are several different places along this stretch of Fillmore Street (in addition to Vivande Porta Via) that you might want to stop at for lunch or a snack. If you just want a snack, **Mad Hatter Tea & Cheshire Cheese,** on the left, is just the place. Farther on, at the corner of Clay and Fillmore streets (on the right) is **La Posada** (at No. 2298), a moderately priced Mexican restaurant that serves enormous portions. The green salsa is excellent and so are the margaritas. If you're looking for a menu with gourmet flair, try the **Fillmore Grill** on the left corner of Clay and Fillmore streets. You can have potato leek soup, a variety of inspired pastas, or the Fillmore Grill burger with seasoned french fries on the side. Try the cheesecake or the pecan pie for dessert. Prices here are moderate.

Cross over to the other side of Fillmore Street after you cross Washington Street because **GJ Mureton's Antiques** (at No. 2510) has some stunning pieces, and is really worth a leisurely browse.

Continue up Fillmore Street to Broadway where you'll be greeted by an incredible view of the water beyond the rooftops. Follow Fillmore all the way to Union Street. At the intersection of Fillmore and Union streets you should note that the building at:

15. **3119 Fillmore Street** was the original site of the Six Gallery where Allen Ginsberg gathered with five other poets and hundreds of onlookers to perform his first reading of *Howl* (see Walking Tour 3, stop 10 for details).

Walking to your right east on Union Street you'll be in the area that was originally known as:

16. **Cow Hollow,** so named because of the 30 dairy farms that were here in 1861. Also located in this area was a small pond known as Washerwoman's Lagoon, the city's primitive laundromat. However, in the latter part of the 19th century pollution from the slaughterhouses, tanneries, and meat-packing factories forced the city to close the dairies. Farms were never allowed in the city again, and the polluted lagoon was filled in with sand.

Since the 1950s, around the time the Beat poets held their readings at the Six Gallery, Union Street has evolved into a shopper's delight, and if you go right on Union Street from the corner of Fillmore Street you'll find seven blocks of boutiques, specialty shops, bookstores, and art galleries. Many of them are housed in some fine old Victorian homes. When you get to the intersection of Buchanan Street you'll see No. 2040 on your left. Although it's now a mini-complex of shops, galleries, and a restaurant (L'Entrecote de Paris), it was one of the original Cow Hollow farmhouses.

As you walk along, stop and take a look at the last stop on the tour, the:

17. **Octagon House** at the corner of Union and Gough streets. It was built in 1861 and is now a museum and home to the National Society of Colonial Dames. The house was built at a time when it was rumored that people would be healthier if they lived in octagonal spaces, and although it makes for interesting architecture, there was never any proof that this claim was true.

If you're here on a day when the house is open you should go inside because it is interesting to see how the space has been divided up. Bedrooms and major living spaces are square, and the leftover triangular spaces serve as bathrooms and closets.

Unfortunately, the house is only open on the second Sunday and second and fourth Thursday of every month between noon and 3pm.

JAPANTOWN & THE WESTERN ADDITION

Start: Corner of Geary Boulevard and Gough Street.

Public Transportation: The 38L bus will take you right to the corner of Geary Boulevard and Gough Street; and the 42, 47, or 49 bus will take you within two blocks of the starting point.

Finish: Fulton between Baker and Broderick streets.

Time: 3 to 4 hours, depending on how long you spend in shops.

Best Times: Between 10am and 5pm during the week when Nihonmachi Mall is open and the neighborhoods are active.

Worst Times: Before 10am or after 5pm.

Hills That Could Kill: None.

Nihonmachi, or Japantown, is bounded loosely by Octavia, Geary, Fillmore, and Pine streets. It's a compact community like Chinatown, and some of the edifices have Asian-style facades, but that is where the similarities end. The Japanese emigrated to the United States much later than the Chinese and in much smaller numbers. It wasn't until the 1868 Meiji revolution that the Japanese were permitted by their government to emigrate. In the 1870s a small number made their way beyond Hawaii (where most Japanese immigrants settled at that time) to San Francisco. More followed after the implementation of the Chinese Exclusion act in 1884. By 1890 the Japanese population numbered 2,000. They took agricultural and horticultural jobs, and some were able to buy land and hire their own workers. The largest number immigrated between 1901 and 1908, and by 1910 the Japanese population in San Francisco numbered over 4,500.

Initially they settled in Chinatown and South of Market Street along Stevenson and Jessie streets from Fourth to Seventh streets. After the 1906 earthquake SOMA became a light industrial area, and the largest concentration of Japanese took root in the Western Addition between Van Ness and Fillmore streets, the site of today's Japantown. By 1940 Japantown covered 30 blocks.

Despite the fact that Japan had been a major contributor to earthquake relief in 1906, the Japanese, like the Chinese, became the subject of ethnic hatred. An Asiatic Exclusion League had been formed in 1905, and the hostility intensified in 1906 when Japanese children were expelled from the public school system. In response, the Japanese refused to send their children to the segregated Asian schools that had been organized and in a secret agreement President Roosevelt agreed to let them attend public schools if the Japanese government cut off all emigration. The 1913, Alien Land Law depriving Japanese Americans the right to buy land, was passed. From 1924 to 1952 Japanese immigration was banned by the United States.

With the Japanese attack on Pearl Harbor anti-Japanese prejudice turned into hysteria. The U.S. government froze Japanese bank accounts, interned community leaders, and removed 112,000 Japanese Americans—two thirds of them U.S. citizens—to camps in California, Utah, and Idaho. Japantown was emptied of Japanese and their places were taken by war workers.

Upon their release in 1945, the Japanese returned home to find their old neighborhood occupied. Most of them resettled in the Richmond and Sunset districts; some did return to Japantown, which had shrunk to a mere six blocks. In 1952, a non-racist Immigration and Naturalization Act was passed, and Asian immigration once again increased. In the '50s Japantown was redeveloped, resulting in what you'll see on your visit today. There is still a concentration of Japanese restaurants, shops, and religious buildings here, and the area is primarily inhabited by Japanese Americans, but the stucco buildings of this neighborhood do not reveal the lives of their inhabitants the way the buildings in Chinatown do. You really have to go inside establishments to find the Asian influence.

The first half of the walk will take you to the Zen and Konko missions and into Nihonmachi Mall (with a few non-Japanese stops as well). It is interesting to compare Japantown with Chinatown, but it's even more interesting to note the American influence on the Japanese community that has gathered here.

• • • • • • • • • • • • • • • •

The first stop on this tour is:

1. **St. Mary's Cathedral.** Although it has virtually nothing to do with Japantown (except that it exists on the outskirts of the area designated as Japantown), it's an interesting stop because of its extraordinary modern architecture.

    After a fire in 1962 destroyed the more traditionally designed cathedral on Van Ness Avenue, a plan for its re-construction was conceived, and the church you see today begun. Completed in 1971, the present cathedral, almost startlingly white, was constructed in the shape of a Greek cross and was the first cathedral to be built after the reforms of the Second Vatican Council in 1962. The incredible cupola is constructed of four 190-foot-high hyperbolic paraboloids, and is best viewed from the interior (if there are no services in progress). Go inside and stand directly under the center of the cupola for the best view of the innovative architecture. Note also the long, narrow stained-glass windows that fill the spaces between each of the paraboloids.

    As you walk around the interior notice the interesting poured concrete organ pedestal and the baldachino by Richard Lippold that hangs above the gold cross over the altar.

    Exit the cathedral and go left on Gough Street past Geary and Post streets to Sutter Street. Go left again, and when you get to Octavia Street, go right to Bush Street. On your right you'll see:

2. **Green's Eye Hospital,** built in 1915 on the site of the former mansion of Thomas Bell, a wealthy pioneer. The only remaining part of the Bell estate is the eucalyptus trees out front. Legend has it that they were planted by Bell's maid, "Mammie" Pleasant (born Mary E. Williams), a suspected voodoo priestess. As long as the eucalyptus trees stand the story of Mary Pleasant and Thomas Bell will be forever woven into the fabric that is San Francisco's history.

Mammie Pleasant was described by Robert O'Brien in *This Is San Francisco* as being "one of the most picturesque and sinister of all San Franciscans." Born in Philadelphia on August 19, 1814, she was placed with the Hussey family in Nantucket at the age of six. She later moved to Boston, where she met and married James W. Smith, a Cuban who was dedicated to the Abolitionist cause. After his death in 1844 she married one of his overseers, John J. Pleasant, and they sailed to California. John Pleasant seems to have disappeared when they arrived in San Francisco because there is no further mention of him in Mary's history.

Her reputation as an incredible cook preceded her to San Francisco. Before she steped off the ship, merchants were waiting, lined up with bids that ranged all the way to $500 a month for her services as a cook. She didn't accept any of them. Instead, she opened a brothel disguised as a boardinghouse at Dupont and Washington streets. Many of the city's highest officials and most respected citizens stayed at her "boarding house" at one time or another. She seemed to wield a mysterious influence over many senators, judges, and wealthy Nob Hill residents, who would become extremely uneasy when she approached.

Twenty-five years after her arrival in San Francisco she moved into the Bell household as their maid, and it quickly became obvious that Mary had complete control over Thomas Bell. He built the house to her specifications and put her name on the title. He also gave her carte blanche for household expenses (for which she spent upwards of $3,000 a month). Neighbors and acquaintances who knew that Mary's mother was from Louisiana (the voodoo capital of the United States) thought that Mary had put a voodoo spell on the Bell family.

Japantown & the Western Addition

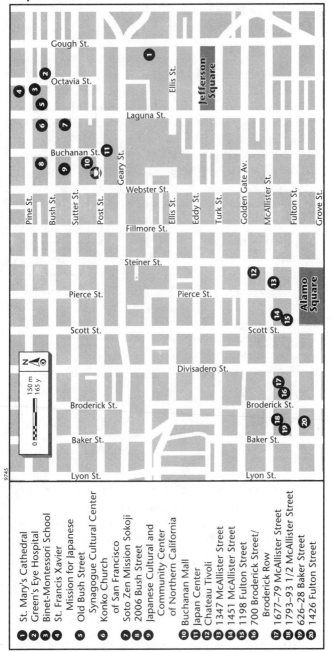

The night of October 16, 1892, Thomas Bell was heard to cry out, "Where am I?" before plunging to his death from the second-floor landing in his own house. No one knows how or why he fell, but Mammie Pleasant's red carriage-driving blanket was found at his side, and many people believed that she pushed him to his death. The bizarre circumstances surrounding Thomas Bell's death did nothing to dispel the citizens' fears of her, though she remained on with Theresa Bell until 1899, when she was finally forced to leave. She died in 1904 and will be forever known as Mammie Pleasant, San Francisco's own voodoo queen.

Continue along Octavia Street. Just before Pine Street on your left look for the:

3. **Binet-Montessori School,** at 1715 Octavia Street, formerly the Morning Star Church, built in 1929. The school's unique facade incorporates a traditional Japanese roof with upturned corners. One detail that stands out is the Madonna and Child in the niche above the front door between the second and third levels of the school.

Across the street at 1710 Octavia Street is the Buddhist Churches of America. Located on the second floor is The Buddhist Bookstore, which has a great selection of Buddhist literature. It's supposed to be open Monday through Saturday from 9am to 5pm, but if you're here around lunchtime, you might be out of luck because the person who runs the shop sometimes closes up then.

Walk up to the corner of Octavia and Pine streets. Across Pine, on your left, is the:

4. **St. Francis Xavier Mission for Japanese** at 1801 Octavia Street on your left. Built in the 1930s, this church serves as the city parish for Roman Catholic Japanese Americans, and the stained-glass windows on the interior depict Catholic missionaries who traveled to Asia. A beautiful Japanese garden surrounds the church.

Turn back, and go one block to Laguna Street and go left to the corner of Bush and Laguna streets, where you'll find on your left the:

5. **Old Bush Street Synagogue Cultural Center** at No. 1881, which was built in 1895 and miraculously

survived the earthquake and fire of 1906, but is decaying today. The structure was declared a landmark in 1988. Plans to restore the building and turn it into a museum and exhibition space of Jewish life in the West were announced then, but little has been done to date.

The synagogue has undergone many changes of ownership. In the 1930s the synagogue was sold to some Japanese Buddhists; in the 1940s it was used by Christians; and later it again became a Zen Temple. When it is completely renovated, it is scheduled to be a cultural center focusing on Jewish history in California and the West.

On the opposite corner at 1909 Bush Street is the:

6. **Konko Church of San Francisco.** The Konko, or "teaching of the golden light," religion was founded in 1859 by Ikigami Konko-Daijin and evolved from the tradition of Shintoism. Konko-Daijin was a simple farmer who maintained his faith in the universe, even in the face of extreme suffering and hardship. It was through this devotion that he became aware of *Tenchi Kane no Kami,* the "principle parent of the Universe," and came to believe that Tenchi Kane no Kami exists in all things and that the entire universe is sustained by Tenchi Kane no Kami. Those who worship in the Konko faith are encouraged to learn not through indoctrination, but simply through living with the awareness that there is a universal power. The religion teaches people to come to complete happiness and peace of mind within themselves.

If you go inside the church, you'll notice the wood altar with its bamboo curtains, and over the altar the *yatsu-nami,* the Konko symbol of the golden light.

There are daily meditation services at 7am and prayer services at 10:30am.

Continue along, down Laguna Street to Sutter Street where you'll find the:

7. **Soto Zen Mission Sokoji.** Designed in 1984, this modern Japanese temple was designed primarily for zazen meditation. If you want to come here for meditation on the black and white cushions that are supplied for you, you'll have to arrive between 6:30 and 8:30am or 6:30 and 8:30pm, otherwise you won't get in.

If you turn right on Sutter Street, you'll pass the Japanese American Citizen's League at 1765 Sutter Street, which served as a civil rights organization from the 1930s on and has worked to wipe out American racism towards Japanese and Japanese Americans.

Cross to the other side of Buchanan Street and go right on Buchanan to Bush Street. Go left to:

8. **2006 Bush Street,** on your right. This house is interesting simply for its architectural design and has nothing whatever to do with the Japanese culture. It is one of the many houses that were prefabricated in New England in 1852 and then shipped around Cape Horn.

    Continue on Bush Street, crossing Webster Street. Midway between Webster and Fillmore streets is a small street called Cottage Row, another one of San Francisco's quaint little hidden blocks that's such a treat to find.

    When you reach the end of Cottage Row, go left on Sutter Street back across Webster to 1840 Sutter Street, where you'll find the:

9. **Japanese Cultural and Community Center of Northern California** on your left. Because of its location in the heart of Japantown, this cultural center has become the central location for activities and events that involve the Japanese-American community as well as interested and informed outsiders. The center's goals are to provide public community space to the Japanese Americans in the Bay Area, as well as to preserve and teach traditional Japanese culture to the younger generation of Japanese Americans.

    Classes, lectures, and events are available to all age groups, and they include programs on karate, tai chi classes, Japanese floral art, paper-doll classes, and shiatsu, among others. The cultural center also houses historical archives, but they are only open by appointment.

    Continue along Sutter Street to Buchanan Street and go right on Buchanan to the:

10. **Buchanan Mall** between Post and Sutter streets. There are some interesting shops located along this cobbled block. Before you go into the actual mall, you might want to stop and check out the sweets in Benkyodo Confectioners on your right for a Japanese taste treat.

Some of the shops you might be interested in are Sanko on the left corner of Buchanan and Sutter streets, which has a wonderful variety of sake sets and tea pots; Genji Kimonos and Antiques, which has some stunning kimonos (well out of my price range); and Soko Hardware, which has an array of Japanese cookware, gardening supplies, and other unique items.

Before you leave the mall you might like to sit and contemplate Ruth Asawa's steel fountain (most likely without water). Asawa attended the famed Black Mountain School in North Carolina from 1946 to 1949.

☕ **Take a Break** Before crossing to the Japan Center in front of you at the end of Buchanan Street, go right on Post Street to **Sanppo** at No. 1702. This place serves some of the best Japanese food in San Francisco in very unpretentious surroundings. You can either sit at the big table in the center (which you will most likely be sharing with Japanese Americans on their lunch hour) or a table of your own. You can get sashimi, teriyaki, or tempura. All orders include miso soup, rice, and pickled vegetables. I would suggest going just before or just after traditional lunch hours so you can get a seat. If you can't, though, it's worth a small wait.

After lunch, go back to the end of Buchanan Street, between Post and Geary streets, to the central entryway of:

11. **Japan Center.** Straight ahead of you is the Peace Pagoda, designed by Professor Yoshiro Taniguchi, who is an expert on ancient Japanese architecture. The pagoda's five tiers rise 100 feet above the reflecting pool. There are plans to beautify the area around the Peace Pagoda, which you can see for yourself on the sign here, but so far nothing is being done.

You should enter the actual Japan Center via the building on your right unless you're interested in Japanese fast food and somewhat tacky shops. (You might want to come back here at night for some karaoke fun.)

Shops that are really worth a stop include the Ikenobo Ikebana Society, which has a school, as well as a shop, where you can buy the special Ikebana "vases." Take a trip into the Taiko shop—not only can you get some terrific taiko drum music, but this tiny shop also displays some appealing art by one of the women who works there. And if you really want to pamper yourself, you should stop in at the Kabuki Hot Spring, where you can have a Japanese bath or Shiatsu massage.

Leave Japan Center via Webster Street, going right to Post Street. Then make a left on Post Street to Fillmore Street. Go left again on Fillmore, walking several blocks to Golden Gate Avenue. Go right on Golden Gate Avenue to the next block, which is Steiner Street. (*Safety note:* As you head from the Japantown area into the Western Addition be extremely alert as to what's going on around you—this is not one of San Francisco's safest neighborhoods.)

Western Addition   This half of the walking tour is mostly a Painted Ladies' walking tour. You will see some of the most beautiful houses in San Francisco on this tour.

When parcels of land were subdivided in San Francisco, money-hungry developers divided their land into small lots that were barely big enough for one house, forcing homeowners and builders to look for other ways to make public displays of their class, wealth, and individuality. Victorian architecture was the perfect medium, and architects went wild with it.

They added turrets, pilasters, fluting, lattices, spindle-work, towers, terra-cotta detailing and friezes, dentil work, and garlands—often all on the same facade. The more detailing and ornamentation a house had, the better. Everyone wanted a different design. The flamboyant houses matched the flamboyance of the city's residents.

Because they were constructed primarily of redwood, many of them burned in the fire of 1906. Of those that survived, many were razed either because buyers considered the excessive ornamentation ugly or because they wanted a more modern-looking home. Others were knocked down because they were a potential fire hazard. Not until the 1960s did people begin to realize the beauty of Victorian architecture. It was then that a restoration project was begun.

At 1057 Steiner Street at Golden Gate Avenue is:

12. **Chateau Tivoli,** probably the most stunning Painted Lady in the city, if not the entire world. Built in 1890 in a combination of Queen Anne and French Revival architectural styles, it was originally the home of Daniel B. Jackson, a lumber man from Oregon. The building's name refers to its second owner, Ernestine Kreling, who was the owner of the Tivoli Opera House, a former favorite venue of the famous Tetrazzini.

    During the 1960s the house lost some of its grandeur when the members of a commune who lived here destroyed the interior woodwork, but the present owners have restored the house to its original condition.

    Chateau Tivoli was up for sale at press time, and its future is uncertain, but I hope you will be able to see it in all its magnificence—that is, with all 18 colors in place. Apparently, it took the current owner (who intended to make this incredible home into a bed-and-breakfast inn) almost a year to restore the exterior.

    It's difficult to see here from the sidewalk, but Chateau Tivoli has San Francisco's only patterned roof.

    The gold accents are stunning, particularly atop the front columns. On the chimney next to the front tower (probably best viewed from across the street), you'll notice a small plaster detail, meant to represent Perseus. The friezes (the horizontal bands around the house) are incredibly detailed and each one is different.

    Go left on Steiner Street to McAllister Street, right on McAllister to:

13. **1347 McAllister Street** between Steiner and Pierce streets. Built in 1900, this French neo-baroque building is decked out in more subdued colors (all 11 of them) than Chateau Tivoli, but it also has some wonderful features. You can best appreciate its overall beauty by standing across the street, but if you approach the front of the house, note one of the most spectacular features of this home—the dome over the front door. Pure elegance, the gold-trimmed woodwork crowns a stained-glass doorway.

    The plaster gods at either side of the windows on the third floor and the ones that flank the two oval windows on the fourth floor are a few of the features that make this house so special.

Continue along McAllister Street to:

14. **1451 McAllister Street.** Reminiscent of the narrow row homes in Amsterdam because of its false gable, this stick-style home was built in 1889. Its owners have created a playful looking structure out of a less-than-playful style of architecture by using bright blue, red, and mustard accents on a dark brown background.

The way the colors have been used helps to accentuate the intricate woodwork—the fluting on the columns, the hand-turned spindles on the stairs leading up to the house, the red framed windows, and the dentil work over the windows on the second floor.

At the corner of Scott Street go left to the corner of Scott and Fulton streets and look for:

15. **1198 Fulton Street,** an Italianate, stick-style home, built in 1882. Characteristic of stick-style architecture are the rectangular bay windows like the ones you see here. The architect's combining of stick-style windows and a flat-front facade typical of Italianate architecture makes this one of the statelier homes you'll see on this tour. One of the building's extra special features is the square tower on the right side of the edifice.

This building has an interesting history. One of its owners, John Mahoney, added the very first garage in San Francisco to the structure, and after him, the house became the White Russians Community Center. Later, during the 1960s, it became a rooming house; Ken Kesey resided here. The house is even featured in Tom Wolfe's *The Electric Kool-Aid Acid Test*. Known today as the Westerfield Mansion, it is a registered historic monument.

From Scott Street, go right on Fulton Street to the corner of Broderick Street. First notice the house at:

16. **700 Broderick Street,** with its refreshing Mediterranean color scheme. Be sure to notice the intricate detailing on the chimney.

The house at 700 begins one of San Francisco's most famous rows of houses. It's known as Broderick Row, and it runs the length of the 700 block.

It was typical for Queen Anne–style houses to be built in rows like this one. The house across the street from 700

Broderick Street also has a finely detailed chimney, as well as a handsome door treatment and curved balustrade above the front door. Its light color scheme, punctuated by darker shades of blue and red, accentuates the house's lovely details.

The house at 704 Broderick Street has a very similar (though less elaborate) door treatment, with a more angular balustrade. Number 708 is another elegant, but more classically designed structure. The woodwork around the windows is especially notable.

Note the oddly shaped roofline on the house at No. 710. It almost looks as though the top might fly right off the house because the bottom floors are so grounded by the brick staircase that leads up to the front door.

Continue up Broderick Street, go right on McAllister Street to:

17. **1677–79 McAllister Street.** This is one of my favorites because of its unabashedly bold color schemes. Painted with colors one would normally never think to combine and built in 1889 in San Francisco–stick style, this house displays a riot of architectural details, such as the decorative "silver dollars" on the first floor.

Turn around, crossing Broderick Street, and follow McAllister Street to:

18. **1793–93½ McAllister Street,** another San Francisco stick-style home, built in 1901 and exquisitely restored and handsomely painted. Some of its special features are the marbleized columns that flank the front door, the marbleized panels above the front door and the second-floor windows, as well as the owl that tops the finial on the left side of the facade. The gold leaf and the stained glass at the front door add a finished, classic touch. The builder left some identifying marks which include the martini glass cut-outs on each of the pillars on the front porch.

Go left on Baker Street to:

19. **626–28 Baker Street,** another example of San Francisco stick style, but in a different form than others you've seen on this tour. It seems somewhat dwarfed by its next-door neighbors; nonetheless, it's an architectural beauty. In particular, note the way the fencing in front of the house

complements the railing along the stairs and at the front of the porch. Note the pineapples on the roof above the bay window on the right side of the house.

Continue on Baker Street, go left on Fulton Street to the last stop on the tour:

20. **1426 Fulton Street.** Another Queen Anne–style home, this one has a gorgeous composition. With its bay windows confined to one side of the house and the front door on the other side, there's a sense of balance. The balcony above the front door increases the sense of balance because it reflects the geometry of the bay windows. Further, there's a welcoming and inviting feeling about the way the stairway leads directly and smoothly to the front door.

If you continue on Fulton Street, you can make a left on Divisadero Street, walking several blocks north back to Post Street. There you can catch the 2, 3, or 4 bus back toward Union Square. Or you can simply return to the Japan Center via Fillmore Street, where it should be a simple matter to get a taxi or some other form of transportation to your next destination.

GOLDEN GATE PARK

Start: At the "Panhandle entrance" (the park's John F. Kennedy Drive) and Stanyan Street.

Public Transportation: The 7, 21, 33, and 71 buses will all take you within two blocks of the starting point.

Finish: 19th Avenue and Cross Over Drive.

Time: 3 to 4 hours, depending on how long you spend in the park's various museums.

Best Times: Sundays, when the main drag of the park (John F. Kennedy Drive) is closed to traffic between Kezar Drive and Transverse Drive.

Worst Times: None.

Hills That Could Kill: None.

The onset of the Gold Rush forced San Francisco to grow quickly, and greed-driven real-estate barons bought land so fast that no one had much time to think about reserving open spaces for the public. Not until the late 1860s did city officials realize the necessity for a sizeable public park where residents could go to escape the bustle of San Francisco's increasingly crowded streets. Around 1870 they chose a piece of land located on the outer edge of the city for the creation of the city's major park. Primarily sand dunes, this land was three miles long and half a mile wide. No one, it seems, anticipated the challenge the dunes and wind would present to a landscape artist.

In 1871, William Hammond Hall was appointed to the position of park superintendent. Hall worked for five years planning out the park's layout, which included curved roads that would encourage people and carriages to move casually and slowly through the park. He resigned in 1876, without having accomplished much more than that.

Although some people were beginning to frequent the park for lack of anywhere else to spend their leisure time, no one in San Francisco at that time expected much to come of it. Eleven years after Hall resigned, the park looked much the same as it did when he left.

Then, in 1887, John McLaren arrived on the scene. Once a student and gardener's helper at London's Royal Botanic Gardens, McLaren followed his heart to the temperate climate of San Francisco where he could create beautiful gardens and plant thousands of trees.

Soon after he arrived in San Francisco, city officials hired him to landscape the park because he had just developed a new strain of grass called "sea bent," which he had planted to hold sandy soil along the Firth of Forth. He agreed to take on the project under four conditions. First, he needed $30,000 a year for planting. Second, he wanted all the water he would need. Third, he wanted the daily sweepings of horse manure from the streets to use as fertilizer. And fourth, there were to be no "Keep Off the Grass" signs. They agreed, but didn't really think he could do the job.

They laughed when he built two windmills for pumping water at the park's ocean edge because they thought he was pumping salt water. But he wasn't. They laughed when he planted the "sea bent" and some other seedlings because they thought they would never take root. But they did. They chuckled to themselves when he planted some rhododendrons, and then began to think he might be on to something. And he was.

It took about 10 years before Golden Gate Park really began to take shape, but there was another problem—the waves that kept sweeping the far end of the garden out to sea. Slowly but surely McLaren was able to solve that problem too by placing bundle after bundle of sticks on the beach so that each time the waves came up they would cover the sticks with sand. Each time they were covered he put more out, and together McLaren and the ocean built a wall between the waves and his park. It took them 40 years, but today that wall is topped by the highway that runs along the ocean side of the park.

Forty years is a long time to spend building a natural wall, and most of us probably would have given up long before the wall even became a bump on the beach, but McLaren had the patience of a saint—except when it came to the statues city officials insisted upon placing all over his park. He called them "stookies," and they drove him crazy. In fact, every time they put up a new one, he planted trees and shrubs and flowers to hide them. The statues are still there, but if you want to see them you're going to have to hunt just a little, because as McLaren intended, many of them are fairly well hidden.

In the 1890s Golden Gate Park hosted the San Francisco Midwinter Exposition, and today you can still see some of the structures that remain from that world's fair, including the Japanese Tea Garden and the Music Stand.

John McLaren cared for the park for 50 years and was loved by all San Franciscans for his lifetime contribution to the city of his dreams. Today the trees planted by John McLaren have grown to heights he could have never envisioned, and beneath them sit the scores of people who flock to the park on sunny days.

This walking tour will take you through the Conservatory of Flowers, into several museums, and to Stow Lake where you can rent a rowboat and relax.

You can also participate in numerous other activities in the park, including archery, tennis, handball, horseback riding, lawn bowling, and horseshoe tossing (don't forget to bring your own horseshoes). Take your time, relax, and by all means, walk on the grass.

• • • • • • • • • • • • • • •

To your right as you enter you'll see the:

1. **McLaren Lodge and Park Headquarters.** This building was the home of John McLaren from the time it was erected until his death in the early 1940s. You can pick up

some information here about this park as well as other parks and recreation areas in San Francisco; it's open Monday through Friday during regular business hours.

Go back to John F. Kennedy Drive and go right. As you walk, go to the left side of the street and take the path that's located diagonally across from Conservatory Drive East. Notice the two statues as you walk along this path. The first is of General Henry W. Halleck, Abraham Lincoln's Civil War chief of staff, who was also responsible for the building of the Montgomery Block (see Walking Tour 3, stop 2).

The next statue you'll see is a charming rendering of an 1880s baseball player sculpted by Douglas Tilden. As you continue along this path you'll come back out onto John F. Kennedy Drive. Across the street you'll see the elegantly designed entrance to the:

2. **Conservatory of Flowers,** built in 1878. This is the oldest building currently in existence in the park. As you head up to the temperature-controlled gardens inside you'll see a statue of former President Garfield on your right. Go around to the right of the building and you'll find yourself in a small but spectacular outdoor garden.

James Lick, the real estate baron, commissioned an Irish company to build this incredible glass house and ship it to San Francisco; unfortunately he didn't live to see its completion.

Go back around to the front, enter the conservatory (there's an admission fee), and head past the souvenir shop in the entryway into the room with the great dome (which was destroyed by fire in 1883 and later rebuilt). You'll find a collection of tropical plants and an incredible orchid display in here. In other parts of the conservatory you'll find seasonal flowers, as well as a lily pond.

When you exit the conservatory, head back out to John F. Kennedy Drive and continue along. As you walk you'll more than likely encounter a group of roller skaters—not the newfangled in-line skaters, the old-fashioned kind—who frequent an area on your right.

Before you get to the 8th Avenue exit, head down a narrow path on your right. It will lead you to the old:

Golden Gate Park

1. McLaren Lodge and Park Headquarters
2. Conservatory of Flowers
3. Powell Street Railroad Station
4. M. H. de Young Museum
5. Asian Art Museum
6. Japanese Tea Gardens
7. California Academy of Sciences
8. Strawberry Hill
9. boathouse

3. **Powell Street Railroad Station,** which was used from 1888 to 1906 to bring visitors to the park by steam train.

    Go back out to John F. Kennedy Drive and go left down Hagiwara Tea Garden Drive. On your right you'll see the bust of Miguel de Cervantes. The sculpture to your left is of Padre Junipero Serra, "Franciscan Father of the California Missions" (see Walking Tour 12, stop 15 for more details).

    Go left between the two concrete sphinxes that flank the entrance to the:

4. **M. H. de Young Museum,** San Francisco's Fine Arts Museum, which opened in 1919. The museum actually grew out of the California Midwinter International Exposition of 1894, which was held in Golden Gate Park. The International Exposition was the brainchild of Michael de Young, and the profits that came from the fair were used to create a collection of art which makes up part of the current collection.

    Inside, you'll find American paintings, sculptures, and decorative arts. Among the artists represented are Mary Cassatt, James McNeill Whistler, John Singer Sargent, and Louis Comfort Tiffany.

    The bookstore has a good collection of books, postcards, cards, and museum replicas.

    From inside the M. H. de Young Museum head into the:

5. **Asian Art Museum of San Francisco,** which opened in 1966 after Avery Brundage, a Chicago insurance man, donated his personal collection to the city of San Francisco. This collection of Asian art, one of the country's finest, is so extensive that it must be rotated; the museum's display space is not large enough for all of it.

    The first floor exclusively displays works from China, while the second floor houses works from Tibet, Japan, Korea, India, Burma, Thailand, Indonesia, Vietnam, and Cambodia. If you're interested in the art of the East, plan on spending a great deal of time here. Leave the museum the way you entered and go right, passing the Pool of Enchantment, which features a small Indian boy playing his pipe to two mountain lions. Continue along, also passing the two marble Chinese lion cubs (also part of Avery Brundage's collection). Soon, on your right, you'll come to the:

6. **Japanese Tea Gardens.** Don't miss these gardens—they're perfectly charming and are well worth the small entrance fee. The gardens, like many of the park's landmarks, were developed for the California Midwinter Exposition of 1894. The buildings within the gardens were the only ones McLaren left standing after the Exposition ended.

John McLaren planted countless trees, bushes, and flowers in Golden Gate Park, but he isn't responsible for the flora here. In 1885, he hired the Hagiwara family to care for the gardens. It is said that the fortune cookie was invented here by the Hagiwaras and introduced to San Franciscans and the world. You can stop in the Tea House for tea and fortune cookies if you're in need of refreshment. There's a tacky gift shop, but it's the only tacky aspect of the gardens.

As you walk among the bonsai and cherry trees, flowers, and over bridges that cross pools of clear, still water, you'll come across a bronze Buddha, cast in Japan in 1790 and donated to the park by the famous Gump family. (For more about the Gumps see Walking Tour 1, stop 13.) You'll also find yourself standing in front of a wonderful tiered, wooden shrine called the Shinto Pagoda. If you have a good sense of balance, don't leave without crossing the Wishing Bridge (those who are at all timid should just go around the bridge—you might just end up wishing you hadn't climbed it in the first place). If you look in the water below the bridge you'll find that the bridge's reflection gives you the illusion that the bridge is a full circle, rather than a half circle.

Come out of the Japanese Tea Garden, cross Hagiwara Tea Garden Drive, passing the Temple of Music on your left. Head around to the left, passing the bronze bust of Beethoven. You'll find the:

7. **California Academy of Sciences** to your right. The academy, which faces the de Young Museum, was founded in 1853 and is the oldest scientific institution in the American West.

Within this building are three institutions—the Halls of Natural History, the Morrison Planetarium, and the Steinhart Aquarium. The aquarium houses a spectacular collection of fish, some penguins, alligators, snakes, dolphins, and seals. One of the most interesting features of the aquarium is the Fish Roundabout—where visitors are completely surrounded by a circular, 100,000 gallon tank. There is also a tropical coral reef.

The Morrison Planetarium presents a variety of sky shows that change throughout the year, and there is a Laserium that presents music and laser light shows.

The Halls of Natural History are of particular interest because they hold some wonderful dioramas. The Wattis Hall of Human Cultures is an anthropological display, showing how different human cultures have adapted to their environments. In the Hohfeld Earth & Space Hall, you can experience the Safe-Quake—a simulation of two of San Francisco's earthquakes. There's also a gallery that features cartoonist Gary Larson's very funny perspective on science.

Exit the Academy of Sciences and go to the left—the direction from which you came to the academy. If you're a lover of Shakespeare, you should go left when you get to Martin Luther King, Jr., Drive and take the first major pathway to your left. You'll soon find on your right the Shakespeare Gardens, founded in 1928, which feature a huge number of the plants mentioned in Shakespeare's plays and sonnets.

Come back out of the gardens and retrace your steps to Martin Luther King, Jr., Drive. Go right and follow it to the Friend's Gate (which will be on your left). Go right and you'll be facing the Japanese Tea Gardens again. Go left until you get to the main intersection of the road that runs around Stow Lake. Go right at the fork and then go left onto the smaller pathway that runs closer to the lake. Continue straight ahead until you get to the Roman Bridge. Cross over the bridge and you'll be on:

8. **Strawberry Hill,** a 430-foot-high man-made island. From up here you can see all over the park. Also up high on the island is a reservoir that used to be the storage place for the park's water and Huntington Falls. If you go down the other

side of the hill and go left on the path that encircles the island you'll come to the Chinese Pavilion, which was a gift to the park from the city of Taipei.

If you still have some energy left after having explored the island, head around the island from the Chinese Pavilion to the Rustic Bridge. Cross the bridge and go right around the other side of the lake until you get to the:

9. **boathouse,** where you can rent pedal, electric, and row boats for a quick or leisurely spin around the island. Stow Lake is the biggest lake in the park, and many people gather at its edges for picnics—there's even a snack bar located here.

To exit the park, get back on the road that encircles the lake, and go left to the first path on your right from the boathouse. Go left when you get to Cross Over Drive and continue walking to the exit on 19th Avenue.

CIVIC CENTER

Start: Grove Street at Market Street.

Public Transportation: 5 or 9 bus, or the K, L, or M Muni to Civic Center Station.

Finish: McAllister Street between Van Ness and Polk streets.

Time: 2 hours.

Best Times: Wednesdays between 8am and 5pm.

Worst Times: Weekends, when many buildings are closed.

Hills That Could Kill: None.

When the nationwide City Beautiful movement began at the turn of the century, San Francisco city planners were excited by the idea of laying out a formal plan for their young city. They sought out David Burnham, a Chicago architect, and asked him to draw up plans.

When Burnham arrived in 1903, he went to work atop Twin Peaks, the best vantage point from which to view the entire city. He studied and planned and sketched for two years, finally emerging with a plan that would make the Civic Center the city's center, from which major boulevards would branch out as they do at Paris's Rond Point.

The Burnham plan was never implemented, but the Civic Center, which was razed by the earthquake of 1906, was rebuilt according to City Beautiful specifications. Designed by Arthur Brown, Jr., and John Bakewell, Jr., what you will see today is the most beautiful beaux-arts complex in the United States.

• • • • • • • • • • • • • • • •

At the corner of Fulton and Market streets is:

1. **United Nations Plaza,** constructed as a memorial to the signing of the United Nations Charter, which took place in San Francisco in 1945.

   If you've scheduled your visit for Wednesday or Sunday between 7am and 5pm you'll be able to enjoy the Heart of the City's Farmer's Market. Much of the produce sold here, though not all, is uniquely Asian.

   Walk through UN Plaza to Leavenworth Street. There, turn left onto McAllister and walk to Hyde Street and the entrance to the:

2. **San Francisco Public Library.** Surfaced with California granite, this library was completed in 1917 at a cost of $1 million. As you enter the main doors, note the five roughly hewn statues in the gallery above the doors. They are obviously unfinished, and it is said that they were set there temporarily until statues of literary figures like Bret Harte, Ina Coolbrith, and Mark Twain could be completed and placed there in the stead of the unfinished works. The project was never completed, so the temporary statues were never taken down.

   If you take a trip up to the third-floor San Francisco History Room and Special Collections Department, you'll find a glass case that holds photographs and other San Francisco memorabilia. The library is open Monday to Saturday; the History Room is open Tuesday, Wednesday, and Friday afternoons and all day on Thursday and Saturday.

   In the Humanities Room and the Main Library Reference Room you'll find two murals by Frank Vincent Dumond, painted in 1914 for the Panama-Pacific International Exposition. They're entitled *Pioneers Leaving the East* and *Pioneers Arriving in the West.*

   Many of San Francisco's famous academics spent time doing research here, among them Eric Hoffer, who came here during the 1930s. Because of Hoffer's childhood blindness (which disappeared when he was 15), he never went to school. After he regained his sight he educated himself at various public libraries around California.

There are plans to move the library to another location in 1996. After that the Asian Museum, which is currently housed in a wing of the M. H. de Young Memorial Museum in Golden Gate Park, will move to this location.

When you exit the library, walk down to Fulton Street, then to:

3. **Civic Center Plaza,** the center of which is lined with flags from other nations. It was originally a lot more appealing to people-watchers than it is today. Gertrude Atherton described it in *My San Francisco:*

> *San Francisco may have her eyesores but is redeemed by her beauty spots, and the Civic Center is one of them. Here there are really noble buildings. The wide plaza with its fountain, its acacia trees and boxed yews is surrounded irregularly by the splendid City Hall, the Public Library, the Civic Auditorium, the State Building . . . the State Building Annex, and those twin structures, the Veterans' Building and the Opera House.*

Today San Francisco's homeless population gathers here daily in silent protest and the grounds are littered with cans, bottles, and candy wrappers.

Go through the park to:

4. **City Hall,** which is directly in front of you. This incredible structure was first conceptualized by the architects at Bakewell and Brown, who entered their design in a competition in the early 1900s. The architects won $25,000; the building itself cost $3.5 million to construct.

The dome was modeled after St. Peter's in Rome and actually rises to a greater height than the dome of the United States Capitol building.

While the outside of the building is stunning, you can't really feel the enormity of it until you go inside. At press time, City Hall was closed indefinitely for a major restoration project, which should take several years. All major city offices have been relocated until this renovation is complete. However, you may still be able to see the bust of

Civic Center

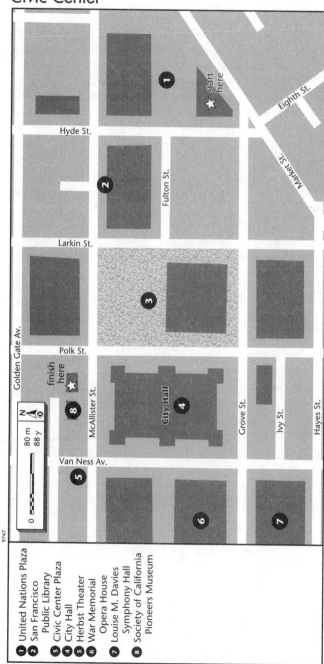

1. United Nations Plaza
2. San Francisco Public Library
3. Civic Center Plaza
4. City Hall
5. Herbst Theater
6. War Memorial Opera House
7. Louise M. Davies Symphony Hall
8. Society of California Pioneers Museum

start here

finish here

N

0   80 m
     88 y

City Hall

Eighth St.

Market St.

Hyde St.

Fulton St.

Larkin St.

Polk St.

Golden Gate Av.

McAllister St.

Van Ness Av.

Grove St.

Ivy St.

Hayes St.

9747

James D. Phelan (1861–1930), a former mayor of San Francisco, in the niche on the left side of the main doors.

The inside of this building, primarily the baroque staircase that leads up to the dome, has been used as a backdrop in many different movies and photographs. Strangely enough many people have had their wedding ceremonies here, including former San Francisco mayor Dianne Feinstein, who was married here in 1980. She invited all the citizens of San Francisco to attend.

Another major event that took place right inside City Hall was the shooting of Mayor George Moscone and supervisor Harvey Milk by disgruntled former supervisor Dan White.

Many of the city's favorite sons have lain in state here, including David Belasco in 1931 (see facing page) and the father of Golden Gate Park, John McLaren, who lay in state for two days in 1943.

Go right on Polk Street to McAllister, and you'll notice the State Office Building on your right diagonally across McAllister Street. As you'll see later, its design compliments the design of the Louise M. Davies Symphony Hall a few blocks down. For now, turn left on McAllister to Van Ness and take note of the:

5. **Herbst Theater** at 401 Van Ness Avenue. Although most agree that this venue is poorly designed, that doesn't stop the shows that go on every night of the year. Murals by Frank Brangwyn decorate the north and south walls of the theater. Titled *Earth, Air, Fire,* and *Water,* they were painted with oil on canvas in 1915 for the Panama Pacific International Exposition and are composed of eight different panels. Inside the theater the United Nations Charter was signed in 1945.

When the theater first opened in 1932, it was called the Veteran's Auditorium, but it was renamed in 1978 after a renovation.

Follow the iron gate in front of the Veteran's Building and it will lead you to the:

6. **War Memorial Opera House,** the home of the San Francisco Performing Arts Center, and of San Francisco's opera and ballet companies. The opera house opened in 1935 as the country's first municipal opera; it seats 3,525.

David Belasco

Actor and playwright David Belasco (1854–1931) and his parents, Humphrey Abraham and Reina Martin Belasco, arrived in San Francisco only a few months after he was born. They found life in San Francisco to be hard and unprofitable, so they moved to Victoria, British Columbia, where David befriended a Catholic priest who encouraged him to exercise his mind. It was in Victoria that he began acting. He was an actor almost from birth, and if he wasn't acting he was haunting theaters all over town.

After the Civil War the Belascos moved back to San Francisco to stay. Life south of Market Street was difficult for David and his family, and to get enough money for food they even had to pawn a gold medal that David had won at school for being the best reader and performer of tragedy.

At 18 he acted in his first paid performance, and at age 29 he headed east to make his fortune. After arriving in Manhattan, Belasco waited 13 years for his first smash hit. Within 10 years after the hit, he was producing plays like *Madame Butterfly* and had opened his own Belasco Theater on Broadway.

Belasco's method for writing a play went something like this: First, he would decide in which period the play would be set. Next he would disappear into his room with a stack of books describing the period. Finally, he would emerge and with the help of a stenographer, who typed out everything he said and another person who kept track of his every movement, he acted out his new play.

San Franciscans loved Belasco, the boy from south of Market Street who made good in New York City. He died of heart failure at age 77.

The opera season begins in September and is then followed by the ballet season. Two opera greats who have graced this stage are Frederica Von Stade and Marilyn Horne (who sang at the inaugural ceremony of President Clinton).

San Francisco's ballet troupe was first organized in 1933 and is the oldest permanent ballet company in the United States. It has won the praise of critics around the world.

Continue along the street past the opera house, crossing Grove Street to the modern:

7. **Louise M. Davies Symphony Hall,** the home of the San Francisco Symphony, which was founded in 1911, and host to top traveling orchestras from around the world. The season runs from October to May. It opened in September 1980 costing $33 million to construct. The hall, which seats 3,000 people, is named after Louise Davies, an arts patron who donated $5 million for its construction. Acoustics are excellent, and the architectural design of the space is such that it allows every person in the hall to have an instrument-level view of the orchestra.

Backtrack on Van Ness Avenue to Grove Street, then turn left. Make a right onto Franklin Street and walk four blocks to Golden Gate Avenue. Another right will bring you back to Van Ness Avenue.

Take a Break   **Modesto Lanzone's** at 601 Van Ness Avenue serves fairly expensive but excellent Italian food. It's open Monday through Friday for lunch, every evening every day except Sunday for dinner. The Hildebrand Lanzone Gallery adjoins the restaurant.

After you've had lunch or a quick browse in the gallery, go right down Van Ness Avenue again. When you get to McAllister Street go left to the:

8. **Society of California Pioneers Museum,** at 456 McAllister Street on the left side of the street. Here you can view some paintings of early California or watch a video that documents the early history of the state. There's also a great library and a stunning collection of Victorian silver displayed in the museum.

The members of the Society of California Pioneers are direct descendants of the original pioneers who came to California in the 1800s.

MISSION DISTRICT

Start: Corner of Army and Dolores streets.

Public Transportation: Muni J-Church to Army Street.

Finish: Dolores and 16th streets.

Time: 3 to 4 hours, not including shopping time.

Best Times: Monday through Saturday from 9am to 5pm.

Worst Times: Before 9am or after 5pm when shops are closed.

Hills That Could Kill: None.

In 1776 the Spanish became the first foreigners to arrive in this neighborhood. Although they left an indelible mark in the form of the adobe Mission Dolores, they had vanished from the scene by the 1800s.

At the beginning of the 19th century, a 40-foot-wide road, similar to a boardwalk, was laid. Soon afterward the area that is now known as the Mission District was quickly filled with gambling houses, saloons, and brothels, as well as farmhouses and private homes. The population grew rapidly and people of many different ethnic groups—Germans, Italians, Americans, and Irish—settled here.

The Mission District is still a multi-ethnic neighborhood, but now you'll find Latinos, American Indians, Asians, Filipinos, and a small community of Irish. It's a bit rougher than some of the other neighborhoods you've visited on these tours, but it holds some of the city's greatest treasures, including a huge number of outdoor murals; Mission Dolores, the city's oldest standing structure; and some handsome Victorian homes. In addition, the Mission District's Valencia Street has become the center of San Francisco's lesbian community.

This tour will take you past some of the Mission District's beautiful Victorian homes, along the ethnic shopping streets, down Valencia Street, and through Balmy Alley with all of its murals, and finally, to Mission Dolores.

● ● ● ● ● ● ● ● ● ● ● ● ● ● ● ●

Walk up one block to 26th Street and go right to Fairoaks Street. Go left on Fairoaks to:

1. **464 and 435 Fairoaks Street.** The former is located on the left side of the street between 25th and 26th streets, and the latter is on the right side of the street, a bit farther down. Both homes were designed by John Coop and are in the San Francisco stick style. Both were also built in 1888.

   You would probably be able to guess that the same architect designed both houses. The buildings share many details, including festooned friezes and woodwork featuring eyelet scalloping over the doors and windows. The woodwork on the sides of the doors and windows have the same cutouts as well. Finally, note the ironwork over the doors—it's original on both houses.

   Walk up to 25th Street and go right to Guerrero Street. Go left on Guerrero to:

2. **1286 Guerrero Street,** which will be on your left. This is a lovely Victorian that was built around 1890 in the Queen Anne style. It has a beautiful tower with a festooned frieze and some very elegant architectural details.

   A bit farther along is another San Francisco stick-style house on your right. Built only a year before No. 1286, this house still has the original iron fence and false gable. Note the tiny flower accents in the woodwork on the bay windows.

   Go right at the corner of 23rd Street to San Jose Avenue. Go right again on San Jose to:

Mission District

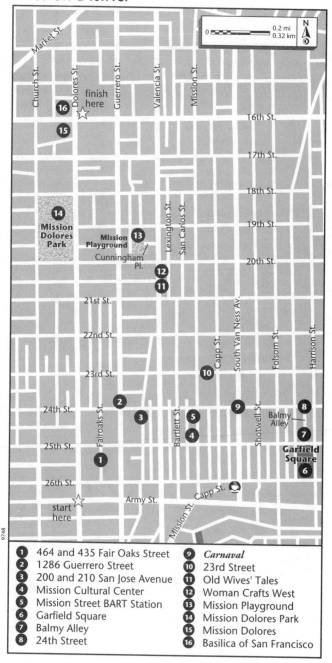

1. 464 and 435 Fair Oaks Street
2. 1286 Guerrero Street
3. 200 and 210 San Jose Avenue
4. Mission Cultural Center
5. Mission Street BART Station
6. Garfield Square
7. Balmy Alley
8. 24th Street
9. *Carnaval*
10. 23rd Street
11. Old Wives' Tales
12. Woman Crafts West
13. Mission Playground
14. Mission Dolores Park
15. Mission Dolores
16. Basilica of San Francisco

3. **200 and 210 San Jose Avenue.** Both houses are Italianate in style, built in 1877 and 1878 respectively. Although both were designed in essentially the same architectural style, No. 210 is more ornate, with Corinthian columns on the front porch. It is also painted in more muted tones than No. 200, probably so that the color wouldn't fight with its more ornate woodwork; you'll notice that the body of No. 200 is done in a bolder shade of purple, probably to dress it up a bit.

Continue down and go left when you get to 25th Street to Mission Street. At Mission Street go left again, and you'll see the:

4. **Mission Cultural Center** on your left. Appropriately, the exterior of the Cultural Center is decorated with a mural that depicts Native American Mexicans. Carlos Loarca, who collaborated with Manuel Villamor and Betsie Miller-Kusz in the painting of the exterior of this building, was one of the first muralists to paint in the Mission. He also taught classes here in the 1970s.

The Mission Cultural Center plays a large role in community activities and organizes a variety of events for the residents of this neighborhood.

Continue along Mission Street, and when you get to 24th Street you'll find the:

5. **Mission Street BART station** on your right, the exterior of which sports a striking mural. Painted in 1975 in politec acrylic, *BART* was done by muralists Michael Rios, Anthony Machado, and Richard Montez.

The imagery of this mural has a slightly disturbing undertone. Androgynous figures support the rails upon which the BART train rides, bending beneath its weight. The train itself, with its angular lead car, appears as a menacing snake. There are masses of the same genderless figures behind the ones that actually hold the tracks. Are they standing, waiting their turn to support the rails themselves, or are they gathered in protest? There's really no way of knowing, although at the time the mural was painted, residents of the neighborhood were worried that because of the new accessibility of the area the cost of living would go up.

Others were happy that they would be able to reach the rest of the city with greater ease than before.

Follow the line of the depicted BART train and you'll see the entrance to the BART station.

Turn around and head back down Mission Street to 26th Street. Go left on 26th and walk to South Van Ness Avenue.

☕ **Take a Break**   **El Cuzcatteco Restaurant,** located on the southeast corner of of the intersection of 26th Street and South Van Ness Avenue, is open daily from 11am to 8 or 9pm and serves inexpensive, enormous portions, mainly to a local crowd. You can get a huge burrito (so big it could be a meal for two), huevos rancheros, and some great traditional fruit drinks that are a taste sensation. If you're not sure of what to order, don't be afraid to ask the server and to try something new. If you're looking for something gourmet, this isn't the place; instead, it's down-home cuisine and decor.

Come back out of the restaurant and go right on 26th Street, following it along to Harrison Street. Go left on Harrison to:

6. **Garfield Square.** Here you'll find several murals. The first will be at 26th and Harrison streets on the right side as you head into Garfield Square. This particular section of the Mission District has a very rough feeling about it, which is evidenced by the graffiti at the base of the mural.

Although most murals are respected by graffiti artists and are left alone, some, tragically, are defaced. I don't know the story behind the mural at Harrison and 26th streets, but some murals are destroyed by neighborhood residents because the neighborhood wasn't consulted in regard to the subject matter or as to its presence at all.

Across the blacktop facing this mural is a community building that houses the public swimming pool, and it is appropriately decorated with oceanic creatures.

Follow Harrison Street to 25th Street and go left to:

7. **Balmy Alley,** where you'll find what must surely be the largest number of murals per square foot in the world.

The mural project in Balmy Alley began unofficially in the late 1970s, but it wasn't until the early 1980s that a group calling itself PLACA (*placa* is a word for a graffiti artist's tag name) came together to paint as many murals as possible on this little street.

In 1983 they began the project (privately funded by people who lived and worked in the Mission District) that monopolized their free time—they worked for free—and resulted in 27 new murals. In 1984 the murals were dedicated with a parade down Balmy Alley.

The murals were restored in 1990.

At the other end of Balmy Alley, at 24th Street, go left. This section of:

8. **24th Street** (all the way to Bryant Street, several blocks to the east) is the heart of the Latino shopping district. You'll find several Latino bakeries, bookstores, and grocery stores.

As you walk along to the left you'll come to the corner of South Van Ness Avenue and 24th Street where, on the left side of the street, you'll find:

9. ***Carnaval,*** another mural, painted in 1983 in oil enamel by muralist Daniel Galvez and others; the artists have cleverly turned this otherwise boring, blank facade and block into a row of beautiful Painted Ladies. To add to the festive feeling created by the jazzy colors used to dress up the faux Victorian homes, the artists added the dancers, drummer, and the crowd gathered "between" the buildings on the left.

Fortunately, this mural has escaped the inevitable destruction faced by most outdoor murals (most likely because of its height and visibility above The House of Brakes, and the clear plastic coating that has been painted over it).

Continue along 24th Street to Mission Street and go right on Mission Street, making a quick detour onto:

10. **23rd Street.** You'll find two more murals here. One simply consists of various types of greenery, while the other, outside the Pathfinder Bookstore, is worth spending some time looking at because each face is distinctly, culturally different. Note also the bookshelves and the flags from varying nations.

Go back to Mission Street and go right, continuing to 22nd Street. Go left on 22nd Street to Valencia Street. Go right on Valencia to:

11. **Old Wives' Tales,** at 1009 Valencia Street on the right side of the street. A women's bookstore that opened in 1977, Old Wives' Tales carries a wide variety of books by and for women—fiction and nonfiction, art books, as well as women's studies and children's books. Men should feel welcome.

    Next door at No. 1007 1/2 is an interesting shop called:

12. **Woman Crafts West,** featuring items that are handmade by women. You'll find jewelry, clothing, and pottery here, among other things. Don't go in thinking you're going to find your average everyday arts and crafts because there are some very unusual, unique, and feminist-oriented pieces. They make great gift items.

    When you've finished shopping and browsing, go right on Valencia Street again. Cross to the other side of Valencia, and when you get to Cunningham Place, go left to the:

13. **Mission Playground,** where you'll find another stunning mural entitled *The New World Tree,* painted in 1987 by Juana Alicia, Susan Cervantes, and Raul Martinez.

    This mural is particularly pleasing not only because of the artists' uses of blues and greens creating a sense of calm for the viewer, but also because they reflect the colors in the sky, grass, trees, and presumably the pool, which lies behind these beautiful walls. If you stand back and squint at the mural, you might feel as though you could walk right into it. The shafts of light that seem to emanate from the center of the building bring the healing element of the sun into the mural.

    The branches of this New World Tree hold a man and boy on one side, a woman and girl on the other. The man and woman are joined together at the top by the baby, which radiates orange light like the sun. All human elements in the painting are of different cultures, and the mural seems to present a new Eden. This new Eden includes other human figures sitting under trees (one man has his hand in the river), forest animals, and a sailing ship.

The mural extends around the side of the building, so do go around and take a look.

Exit the Mission Playground on the north end onto 19th Street. Go left on 19th Street and follow it to Dolores Street. You'll be directly in front of:

14. **Mission Dolores Park,** which was initially two Jewish cemeteries when the land was purchased in 1861. Later, when the cemeteries hampered the city's expansion the remains of most people buried here (and other cemeteries around the city) were exhumed and moved to new cemeteries established well outside the boundaries of San Francisco.

The park, which was laid out in 1905, is the biggest park in the Mission District. (You'll probably think of it more in terms of a plaza than a park because of the presence of so much concrete.)

At the corner of 19th and Dolores streets is a replica of Mexico's Liberty Bell, which was donated in 1962. On the opposite side of the park, on the corner of Church and 20th streets (diagonally across the park from where you stand now) you can enjoy a panoramic view of the city.

After you've absorbed the view, go back to 19th and Dolores streets and continue up (going left out of the park) to 18th Street, where you'll see two more murals on the facade of the Real Good Karma Restaurant.

Continue up Dolores Street to:

15. **Mission Dolores,** at 320 Dolores Street. Officially called Mission San Francisco de Assisi, this was the sixth of 21 California missions established by Father Junipero Serra. The first group of explorers arrived here on June 27, 1776, and the first service was held by Father Francisco Palou two days later under a tent. Palou was responsible for the design of the mission you see today, and he is buried in the cemetery behind the mission.

Building began on this adobe structure in 1782 and was completed in 1791. It has survived all earthquakes and fires that have plagued the city over the years and is the oldest building standing in the city of San Francisco today. Willis Polk helped restore it in 1918, and the building is currently covered with stucco to preserve the adobe and to avoid the enormous annual maintenance costs that would be incurred if the adobe was exposed to the elements.

There's a small fee to see the interior, the cemetery, and the museum, but it's worth it.

Once inside the four-foot-thick walls of the church you'll notice that the air is generally cooler and damper than the air outside. This is because the adobe walls are so thick that they hold the cool air inside. Masses are not regularly held here, but this is the parish baptistry. Have a look at the wonderful Victorian marble font, the painted and gilded altar, and the incredible ceiling.

The painted ceiling and beams are done in a design that the Costanoan Indians (one of the two main tribes of Indians who were the Bay Area's first inhabitants) used. The Costanoans used vegetable dyes for their painting. The altars and statues in the niches came directly from Mexico in the 1880s.

Exit the church on the right side just in front of the altar, and go left through the covered porch where you'll find a series of photographs that show the mission at various stages in its history. Continue around and enter the small museum, which used to be the mission classroom but now holds various artifacts, including the baptismal register that dates from 1776 and some sacred items that were gifts of Father Serra. Note also the wood trusses; they were originally held together by rawhide strips but were given steel reinforcements in 1918 as protection against earthquakes.

Exit the museum, and you'll find yourself in a peacefully landscaped, fountained courtyard. You can sit here and relax if you like before entering the cemetery.

Buried in the cemetery are Costanoan Indians; Spanish, Mexican, and American pioneers; as well as a large number of Irish immigrants who attended services at this parish. It's interesting to walk around the graveyard reading the epitaphs. Charles Cora, hanged by the Vigilante Committee of 1856, is buried here—look for the brown sandstone grave marker embellished with firemen's helmets. Another criminal hanged by the vigilantes, James P. Casey, is also buried in the cemetery. Dignitaries of the church are buried alongside the wall of the church. Among them are Francisco de Haro, the first mayor of San Francisco, and Father Palou.

Go back around, through the courtyard and museum, back to the covered porch. Follow the signs to the:

16. **Basilica of San Francisco,** which is the official parish church. The original building did not survive the earthquake in 1906 and was rebuilt. This structure was completed in 1918.

Not every church has the honorable title "basilica," which can only be conferred to a church by the pope. In 1952 Pope Pius XII designated this building a basilica. The red and gold umbrella and the coat of arms with the papal insignia on the altar are symbols of the church's special status.

Though the interior of this church is less exciting than the mission, it is interesting to note that the windows depict Saint Francis of Assisi (patron saint of the city), and the 21 California missions.

There is a wood carving of Mater Dolorosa, Our Lady of Sorrows, above the main altar. The Seven Sorrows of Mary are shown above the door at the rear and on the side balconies.

ESSENTIALS &
RECOMMENDED READING

This section includes all the basic information you will need to make your stay in San Francisco easier. I'm including a run-down of the layout of the city and transit information to make getting around a lot easier. There's an A-to-Z list of basic information to answer virtually any question you might have. Finally, I've included a short reading list in the event you would like to soak up some of the San Francisco atmosphere before you depart. The city's compact size (only 46 square miles for a city of almost 750,000 people) and moderate climate make it an ideal candidate for strolling around. You'll find the people friendly and the scenery superb. Just show a moderate amount of caution, as you would in any large metropolitan area; ask your hotel staff and the tourist information office if you are in doubt about visiting any particular neighborhood. But most of all, enjoy.

Downtown San Francisco

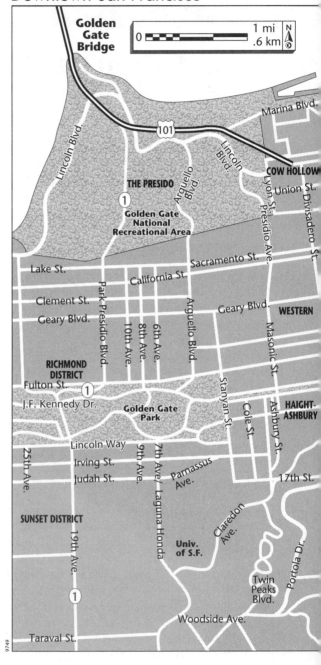

Golden Gate Bridge

101

Marina Blvd.

Lincoln Blvd

THE PRESIDO

Arguello Blvd.

Lincoln Blvd.

Lyon St.

Presidio Ave.

COW HOLLOW

Union St.

Divisadero St.

Golden Gate National Recreational Area

1

Lake St.

Sacramento St.

California St.

Clement St.

Park Presidio Blvd.

10th Ave.

8th Ave.

6th Ave.

Arguello Blvd.

Geary Blvd.

Geary Blvd.

WESTERN

Masonic St.

RICHMOND DISTRICT

Fulton St.

1

J.F. Kennedy Dr.

Golden Gate Park

Stanyan St.

Cole St.

Ashbury St.

HAIGHT-ASHBURY

25th Ave.

Lincoln Way

Irving St.

Judah St.

9th Ave.

7th Ave./Laguna Honda

Parnassus Ave.

17th St.

SUNSET DISTRICT

19th Ave.

1

Univ. of S.F.

Claredon Ave.

Twin Peaks Blvd.

Portola Dr.

Woodside Ave.

Taraval St.

9749

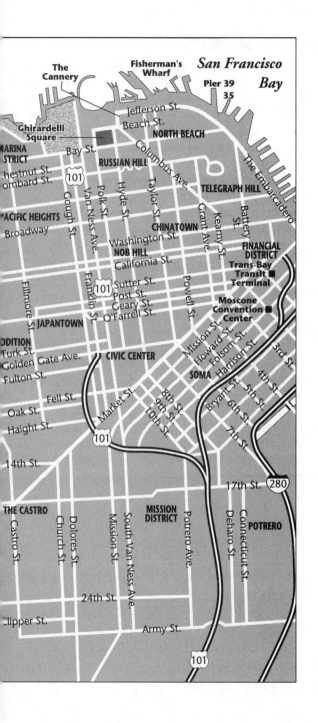

TOURIST INFORMATION

The **San Francisco Visitor Information Center** is located on the lower level of Hallidie Plaza, 900 Market St., at Powell Street (tel. 415/391-2000). They're open Monday through Friday from 9am to 5:30pm, on Saturday from 9am to 3pm, and on Sunday from 10am to 2pm. The staff here can provide you with answers to all your questions. They also have good area street maps and brochures in German, Japanese, French, and Spanish as well as English. To find the office, descend the escalator at the cable-car turnaround.

If you've got extra energy after walking the tours in this book, you can dial 391-2001 any time of day or night for a **recorded message** about current cultural, theater, music, sports, and other special events. This information is also available in German (tel. 391-2004), French (tel. 391-2003), Japanese (tel. 391-2101), and Spanish (tel. 391-2122).

City Layout

San Francisco may seem confusing at first, but it quickly becomes easy to negotiate. The city's downtown streets are arranged in a simple grid pattern, with the exception of Market Street and Columbus Avenue, which cut across the grid at right angles to each other. Hills appear to distort this pattern, however, and can seem disorienting. But as you learn your way around, these same hills will become your landmarks and reference points.

Main Arteries & Streets   Market Street is San Francisco's main thoroughfare. Most of the city's buses ply this strip on their way to the Financial District from the bedroom communities to the west and south. The tall office buildings that create the city's stalactite skyline are clustered at the northeast end of Market; one block beyond lie the Embarcadero and the bay.

The **Embarcadero** curves north along San Francisco Bay, around the perimeter of the city. It terminates at Fisherman's Wharf. Aquatic Park and the Fort Mason complex are just ahead, occupying the northernmost point of the peninsula.

From here, **Van Ness Avenue** runs due south, back to Market Street. The area I have just described forms a rough triangle bounded by Market Street to the east, the waterfront to the north, and Van Ness Avenue to the west. Within this triangle lie most of the city's main tourist sights.

Getting Around

By Public Transportation   The **San Francisco Municipal Railway,** better known as **Muni** (tel. 415/673-6864), operates the city's cable cars, buses, and Metro streetcars. Together, these three public-transportation services criss-cross the entire city, rendering San Francisco fully accessible to visitors who are otherwise vehicularly deprived. Exact change is required on all public transportation except cable cars.

For detailed route information, phone Muni or consult the bus map at the front of the San Francisco *Yellow Pages.* If you plan on making extensive use of public transportation, you may want to invest in a comprehensive route map, sold at the Visitor Information Center (see "Tourist Information," above) and in many downtown retail outlets.

Muni discount passes, called "Passports," entitle holders to unlimited rides on buses, Metro streetcars, and cable cars at reasonable rates, and also entitle you to admission discounts at 26 of the city's major attractions. Among the places where you can purchase a Passport are the San Francisco Visitor Information Center, the Holiday Inn Civic Center, the San Francisco Ticket Box Office Service (STBS) booth at Union Square, and the Cable Car Museum (at Mason and Washington streets).

By Cable Car   San Francisco's cable cars may not be the most practical means of transport, but they are the best loved. They are also official historic landmarks, designated as such by the National Park Service in 1964. There are three lines in all. The most scenic—and exciting—is the Powell-Hyde line, which follows a zigzag route from the corner of Powell and Market streets, over both Nob Hill and Russian Hill, to a turntable at gaslit Victorian Square in front of Aquatic Park. The Powell-Mason line starts at the same intersection and climbs over Nob Hill before descending to Bay Street, just three blocks from Fisherman's Wharf. The California Street line begins at the foot of Market Street and runs a straight course through Chinatown and over Nob Hill to Van Ness Avenue. All riders must exit at the last stop and wait in line for the return trip. The cable-car system operates from approximately 6:30am to 12:30am.

By Bus   Buses reach almost every corner of San Francisco, and beyond—they travel over the bridges to Marin County and Oakland. Some buses are powered by overhead electric cables;

San Francisco Mass Transit

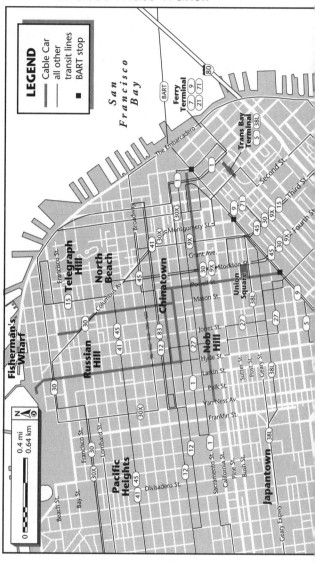

others use conventional gas engines. All are numbered and display their destinations on the front. Stops are designated by signs, curb markings, and yellow bands on adjacent utility poles. Most buses travel along Market Street or pass near Union Square. They

run from about 6am to midnight, after which there is infrequent all-night "Owl" service.

By Metro Streetcar Muni's five Metro Streetcar lines, designated J, K, L, M, and N, run underground downtown and on the street in the outer neighborhoods. The sleek railcars make the same stops as BART (see below) along Market Street, including Embarcadero Station (in the Financial District), Montgomery Street and Powell Street (both near Union Square), and the Civic Center (near City Hall). Past the Civic Center, the routes branch off in different directions: The J line will take you to Mission Dolores; the K, L, and M lines to Castro Street; and the N line parallels Golden Gate Park. Metros run about every 15 minutes—more frequently during rush hours. Service is offered Monday through Friday from 5am to 12:30am, on Saturday from 6am to 12:20am, and on Sunday from 8am to 12:20am.

By BART　BART, an acronym for Bay Area Rapid Transit (tel. 788-BART), is a futuristic-looking, $5-billion high-speed rail network that connects San Francisco with the East Bay—Oakland, Richmond, Concord, and Fremont. Four stations are located along Market Street (see "By Metro Streetcar" above). Tickets are dispensed from machines in the stations and are magnetically encoded with a dollar amount. Computerized exits automatically deduct the correct fare. Children 4 and under ride free. Trains run every 15 to 20 minutes, Monday through Friday from 4am to midnight, on Saturday from 6am to midnight, and on Sunday from 8am to midnight.

By Taxi　Taxis can be hailed on most major thoroughfares. When a cab is available for hire, the sign on its roof will be lighted. If you can, it's best to phone in advance and request a cab to pick you up at a designated location. The following licensed private companies compete for customers: **Veteran's Cab** (tel. 552-1300), **Desoto Cab Co.** (tel. 673-1414), **Luxor Cabs** (tel. 282-4141), **Yellow Cab** (tel. 262-2345), **City** (tel. 468-7200), and **Pacific** (tel. 986-7220). Rates are approximately $2 for each mile.

By Car　Scores of car-rental firms are located in San Francisco, and charge competitive rates. A minimum-age requirement—ranging from 19 to 25—is set by most rental agencies. Some also have a maximum-age limit. If you're concerned that these limits may affect you, ask about rental requirements at the time of booking to avoid problems later.

Some of the national car-rental companies operating in San Francisco include: **Alamo** (tel. toll free 800/327-9633), **Avis** (tel. toll free 800/331-1212), **Budget** (tel. toll free 800/527-0700), **Dollar** (tel. toll free 800/800-4000), **Hertz** (tel. toll free

800/654-3131), **National** (tel. toll free 800/227-7368), and **Thrifty** (tel. toll free 800/367-2277).

In addition to the big chains, there are dozens of regional rental places in San Francisco, many of which offer lower rates. These include **A-One Rent-A-Car,** 434 O'Farrell St. (tel. 415/771-3977); and **Bay Area Rentals,** 440 O'Farrell St. (tel. 415/441-4779).

Parking

Street parking in San Francisco is extremely limited. Parking is particularly tough in Chinatown, around Nob Hill, by Fisherman's Wharf, in North Beach, and on Telegraph Hill. Where street parking is not metered, signs will tell you when you can park and for how long. Curb colors also indicate parking regulations—and mean it! *Red* means no stopping or parking; *blue* is reserved for disabled drivers with a California-issued disabled plate or a placard; *white* means there's a five-minute limit; *green* indicates a 10-minute limit; and *yellow* and *yellow-black* curbs are for commercial vehicles only.

When parking on a hill, apply the hand brake, put the car in gear, and *curb your wheels*—toward the curb when facing downhill, away from the curb when facing uphill. Curbing your wheels will not only prevent a possible "runaway" but will also keep you from getting a ticket—an expensive fine that is aggressively enforced.

Parking lots abound, and are moderately expensive. Parking often costs about $4 to $5 per hour. It's cheaper by the day: from $13 to $20 for 24 hours. In Chinatown the best (and cheapest) place to park is the Portsmouth Square Garage at 733 Kearny St. (enter between Clay and Washington streets). Between 10:30am and 2:30pm you may have to wait in line to enter. At the Civic Center, try for the Civic Center Plaza Garage between Polk and Larkin streets. Downtown, head for the Sutter-Stockton Garage at 330 Sutter St. At Fisherman's Wharf/Ghirardelli Square, try the North Point Shopping Garage at 350 Bay St. or the Ghirardelli Square Garage at 900 North Point. On Union Street, in the area of high-traffic shopping, try the Cow Hollow Garage at 3060 Fillmore St.

Driving Rules

California law requires that both drivers and passengers wear seatbelts. You may turn right at a red light unless otherwise indicated. Cable cars always have the right-of-way, as do pedestrians at intersections and crosswalks.

FAST FACTS **San Francisco**

American Express   For travel arrangements, traveler's checks, currency exchange, and other member services, American Express has offices at 2500 Mason St. (tel. 788-3025), near Fisherman's Wharf (open daily 10am to 6pm), and at 455 Market St. (tel. 512-8250) in the Financial District (open Monday through Friday from 9am to 5pm). To report lost or stolen traveler's checks, call toll free 800/221-7282.

Area Code   There are two area codes in the San Francisco Bay Area. The city of San Francisco and the entire peninsula is identified by the 415 area code. Oakland, Berkeley, and much of the East Bay uses the 510 area code. All phone numbers in this book assume San Francisco's 415 area code, unless otherwise noted.

Business Hours   Banking hours vary, but most **banks** are open Monday through Friday from 9am to 3pm. Several stay open until about 5pm at least one day during the week. Many banks also feature Automated Teller Machines (ATMs) for 24-hour banking.

Most **stores** are open Monday through Saturday from 10am to 6pm; closed Sunday. But there are exceptions: Stores in Chinatown are generally open daily from 10am to 10pm. Ghirardelli Square and Pier 39 shops are open Monday through Thursday from 10am to 6pm and on Friday and Saturday from 10am to 9pm (later during the summer). San Francisco Shopping Center shops are open Monday through Saturday from 9:30am to 8pm and on Sunday from 11am to 6pm. Large department stores, including Emporium, Macy's, and Nordstrom, keep late hours and are open Sunday.

Hours in **restaurants** vary, but most serve lunch from about 11:30am to 3pm and dinner from 5:30 to 11pm. You can sometimes get served later on weekends. **Nightclubs and bars** are usually open daily until 2am, when they are legally bound to stop serving alcohol.

Climate   The Bay Area's temperate marine climate means relatively mild weather all year round. In summer, temperatures rarely top 70°F, and the city's famous fog rolls in most mornings and evenings. In winter, the mercury seldom falls below freezing. But the weather here *is* notoriously unpredictable; no matter what time of year you visit, packing a warm sweater and an all-weather jacket is a good idea.

Currency Exchange   Foreign-exchange bureaus are rare in the United States, and most banks are not equipped to handle currency exchange. San Francisco's money-changing offices include: **Bank of America,** 345 Montgomery St. (tel. 415/622-2451), open Monday through Thursday from 9am to 4pm, and Friday from 9am to 5pm; and **Thomas Cook,** 75 Geary St. (tel. 415/362-3452), open Monday through Friday from 9am to 5pm.

Though **traveler's checks** are widely accepted, make sure that they are denominated in U.S. dollars, as foreign-currency checks are difficult to exchange.

Earthquakes   There will always be earthquakes in California—most of which you'll never notice. However, in case of a significant shaker, there are a few basic precautionary measures you should know. When you are inside a building, seek cover; *do not run outside.* Move away from windows toward the center of the building. Duck under a large, sturdy piece of furniture or stand against a wall or under a doorway. If you exit the building, use stairwells, not elevators. If you are in your car, pull over to the side of the road and stop—but not until you are away from bridges, overpasses, telephone poles, and power lines. Stay in your car. If you're out walking, stay outside and away from trees, power lines, and the sides of buildings. If you're in an area with tall buildings, find a doorway in which to stand.

Emergencies   To reach the police, an ambulance, or fire department, dial **911** from any phone; no coins are needed. Emergency hotlines include the Poison Control Center (tel. 476-6600), Suicide Prevention (tel. 221-1424), and Rape Crisis (tel. 647-7273).

Newspapers/Magazines   The city's two main dailies are the *San Francisco Chronicle* and the *San Francisco Examiner;* both are distributed throughout the city. The two papers combine for a massive Sunday edition that includes a pink "Datebook" section—an excellent preview of the week's upcoming events. The free weekly *San Francisco Bay Guardian,* a tabloid of news and listings, is indispensable for nightlife information; it's widely distributed through street-corner dispensers and at city cafés and restaurants.

Of the many free tourist-oriented publications, the most widely read are *Key* and *San Francisco Guide.* Both of these handbook-size weeklies contain maps and information on current events. They can be found in most hotels and in shops and restaurants in the major tourist areas. Gay and lesbian visitors should seek out the *San Francisco Sentinel* or the *Bay Area Reporter*; both are distributed free.

Safety   Tourists are rarely the victims of violent crime. Still, few locals would recommend that you walk alone late at night. The Tenderloin, between Union Square and the Civic Center, is one of San Francisco's most infamous areas. Compared with similar areas in other cities, however, even this section of San Francisco is relatively tranquil. Other areas where you should be particularly alert are the Mission District, around 16th Street and Mission Street; the Fillmore area, around lower Haight Street; and the SoMa area south of Market Street.

Taxes   An 8.5% sales tax is levied on all goods and services purchased in San Francisco.

Time   San Francisco, like the entire West Coast, is in the Pacific standard-time zone, which is 8 hours behind Greenwich mean time. To find out what time it is, call 767-8900.

Useful Telephone Numbers   **American Express Global Assist** (for cardholders only) (tel. toll free 800/554-2639), **tourist information** (tel. 391-2001), **highway conditions** (tel. 557-3755), **time** (tel. 767-8900), **weather** (tel. 936-1212).

RECOMMENDED READING

Architecture

Bernhardi, Robert C. *Great Buildings of San Francisco* (Dover, 1988).

Larsen, Michael, and Elizabeth Pomada. *The Painted Ladies Revisited* (E. P. Dutton, 1989).

Woodbridge, Sally B., and John M. *San Francisco Architecture* (Chronicle Books, 1992)

Art

Albright, Thomas. *Art in the San Francisco Bay Area 1945–1980* (University of California Press, 1985).

Drescher, Timothy W. *San Francisco Murals: Community Creates Its Muse 1914–1990* (Pogo Press, 1991).

History

Ashbury, Herbert. *The Barbary Coast* (Garden City, 1933).

Atherton, Gertrude. *My San Francisco* (Bobbs-Merrill, 1946).

Bancroft, H. H. *History of California* (Bancroft, repr. of 1900 edition).

Caen, Herb. *Baghdad by the Bay* (Comstock, 1987).

Caen, Herb. *Don't Call it Frisco* (Doubleday, 1953).

Caen, Herb. *Only in San Francisco* (Doubleday, 1960).

Clemens, Samuel L. *Mark Twain's San Francisco* (Greenwood, 1978).

Dana, Richard. *Two Years Before the Mast* (Penguin, 1981).

Dickson, Samuel. *The Streets of San Francisco* (Stanford University Press, 1955)

Genthe, Arnold, and John K. Tchen. *Photographs of San Francisco's Old Chinatown* (Dover, 1984).

Jackson, Pauline. *City of the Golden 'Fifties* (University of California Press, 1941).

Jewett, Masha Zakheim. *Coit Tower: Its History and Its Art* (Volcano Press, 1983).

Jones, Idwal. *Ark of an Empire: San Francisco's Montgomery Block* (Doubleday, 1951).

Lewis, Oscar. *The Big Four* (Comstock Editions, 1971).

Lewis, Oscar. *Mission to Metropolis* (Howell-North Books, 1980).

Lewis, Oscar. *Silver Kings* (Alfred A. Knopf, 1947).

O'Brien, Robert. *This Is San Francisco* (McGraw Hill, 1948).

Perry, Charles. *The Haight-Ashbury: A History* (Random House, 1985).

Riesenberg, Felix, Jr. *Golden Gate: The Story of San Francisco Harbor* (Alfred A. Knopf, 1940).

Shilts, Randy. *The Mayor of Castro Street: The Life & Times of Harvey Milk* (St. Martin's Press, 1988).

Yee, Chiang. *The Silent Traveller in San Francisco* (W. W. Norton, 1964).

Literature

Allen, Donald, ed. *The New American Poetry, 1945–1960* (Grove, 1960).

Bierce, Ambrose. *Devil's Dictionary* (Stemmer House, 1978).

Burgess, Gelett. *The Heart Line* (1907).

Cassady, Carolyn. *Heart Beat* (1976).

Charters, Ann. *Scenes Along the Road* (Gotham Book Mart, 1970).

Ferlinghetti, Lawrence, and Nancy Peters. *Literary San Francisco* (Harper & Row, 1980).

Ginsberg, Allen. *Howl and Other Poems* (City Lights Publishing, 1956).

Hammett, Dashiell. *The Maltese Falcon* (Alfred A. Knopf, 1929).

Herron, Don. *The Literary World of San Francisco & Its Environs* (City Lights, 1985).

Harte, Bret. *The Luck of Roaring Camp and Other Sketches* (Jamestown, 1976).

Kerouac, Jack. *The Dharma Bums* (Penguin, 1971).

Kerouac, Jack. *On the Road* (Penguin, 1976).

Kherdian, David. *Six San Francisco Poets* (Giligia, 1969).

Maupin, Armistead. *Tales of the City* (HarperCollins, 1978).

Miles, Barry. *Ginsberg: A Biography* (Simon & Schuster, 1989).

Norris, Frank. *McTeague: A Story of San Francisco* (Penguin, 1982).

Patchen, Kenneth. *Collected Poems* (New Directions, 1969).

Plummer, William. *The Holy Goof* (1981).

Rath, Virginia. *The Dark Cavalier* (1938).

Rath, Virginia. *A Dirge for Her* (1947).

Tan, Amy. *The Joy Luck Club* (Ivy Books, 1990).

Tan, Amy. *The Kitchen God's Wife* (G. P. Putnam, 1991).

Twain, Mark. *Roughing It* (1873).

Wolfe, Tom. *The Electric Kool-Aid Acid Test* (Farrar, Straus & Giroux, 1987).

INDEX

177